KNOWING
THE VOICE
OF GOD

KNOWING THE VOICE OF GOD

DISCOVER GOD'S UNIQUE LANGUAGE FOR YOU

DIANE EBLE

ZondervanPublishingHouse
Grand Rapids, Michigan

A Division of HarperCollinsPublishers

Knowing the Voice of God
Copyright © 1996 by Diane Eble

Requests for information should be addressed to:

📖 ZondervanPublishingHouse
Grand Rapids, Michigan 49530

Library of Congress Cataloging-in-Publication Data

Eble, Diane.
   Knowing the voice of God: discover God's unique language for you /
Diane Eble.
     p. cm.
   ISBN: 0-310-20192-6 (pbk.)
    1. God—Attributes. 2. God—Knowableness. 3. Spiritual Life—
Christianity.
I. Title.
BT130.E25 1996
231.7-dc 20   95-51503
                                      CIP

Interior design by Sue Vandenberg Koppenol

Printed in the United States of America

96 97 98 99 00 01 02 /❖ DH/ 10 9 8 7 6 5 4 3 2

CONTENTS

Introduction

A Hunger for God

"You can have a personal relationship with God." As a young teenager, when I first heard these words from the lips of a bubbly classmate, I was astounded, intrigued, and a little miffed. It seemed too good to be true. If it were true, why were so many of the religious people I knew so quiet about it? If they really knew the living God, why weren't they jumping for joy and shouting it out?

I think the answer has partly to do with the difference between religion, which is merely knowing *about* God, and true faith or spirituality, which is *knowing* God. True faith is knowing the One True God, who has revealed himself as he wants to be revealed—and continues to reveal himself, on his own terms.

I am an ordinary person who has an extraordinary hunger and thirst for knowing God, and who has begun to find satisfaction for my hunger. I can honestly say that the astounding experience at the heart of several thousand years of biblical history is true for me: I have a personal relationship with the living God. It is like the blood that nourishes every cell of my body. Everything I do or think or say is in some way connected to this relationship I have with God.

Not that I am perfect. Oh no, not a chance. But this relationship allows for my imperfection, just as my relationship with my own children incorporates their disobedience and imperfection. I constantly fail God. But even in failing, I am measuring myself against the standards set by God. I seek his forgiveness and power to change. We are still connected.

God is constantly making himself real to me, and this is the biggest, deepest, most satisfying thrill of my life. I want everyone to come to know God in the same deep, truly personal way.

And here I come up against a paradox that is the essence of this book. The paradox is this: Because God is personal, he reveals himself to each of us in unique ways. But because he is God, wholly Other, wholly sovereign, and over all creation, he is not merely whatever I want to make of him. This is where so much of the current spirituality goes astray. If religion has erred on the side of not allowing God to reveal himself afresh to each generation and each person, "New Age" spirituality has not taken into account God's revelation through the centuries. God becomes a "small god inside," limited to whatever we want to make of him.

I once attended one of the anonymous recovery group meetings in which Steps Two and Three of the Twelve Steps were explained. (Step Two: "Came to believe that a Power greater than ourselves could restore us to sanity." Step Three: "Made a decision to turn our will and our lives over to the care of God *as we under-stood him*.") One of the members explained, "You can call that tree outside the window there your Higher Power. Whatever you want it to be, it can be."

No, I wanted to say. It is not our act of imbuing divine power on an object that makes it divine. It is not our believing that makes something so. It is the objective reality, the existence outside ourselves. The God who acted throughout biblical history, who still promises to act today—that is the God I am coming to know and love and adore.

And so we have this fine line to walk, if we want to truly know God. We can never fully know God (he is too full, too big; we are too limited, too small), yet we must seek him with heart and soul and mind and strength. We need to be totally open to his revelation of himself to us, yet we need to distinguish our own imaginations and longings from the way God truly is.

If you long to know God, my friend, I invite you to begin a journey. I urge you to come with an open mind. With an open mind and an honestly seeking heart, you will find God. He himself promises it: "You will seek me and find me, when you seek me with your whole heart" (Jeremiah 29:13).

STUDYING GOD'S POEM—YOU!

In this book we will explore what it means to "have a personal relationship with God." The Bible says that God longs for us to hear his voice, that he longs for us to delight in his work in our lives. He is constantly at work in our lives, creating a beautiful poem (Ephesians 2:10). But are we reading it? Have we been taught how to read and understand our own poems, how to interpret our own works of art?

I believe the deepest desire of the human heart is to be able to trace the hand of God in our lives day by day, to know that he is as real as the air we breathe, though we can't see him any more than we can see air. I believe that God reveals himself to us as unique individuals, and that we can learn the special "love language" he is whispering in our ears. Just as every human relationship is unique and special because the individuals are each unique, so our relationship with God has an unrepeatable, special aspect to it. The common goal of every Christian's life is "to glorify God and enjoy him forever," but I believe each of us does that in an unrepeatable way. And part of the way we glorify God is through developing a personal relationship with him, hearing the nuances of his work in our lives, and responding to him as only we can. Thus, our task is to learn to atune our ears to the music of the song he is writing through our lives, to train ourselves to understand the subtleties of the poem he is writing in our lives, to understand the principles of color and form and line so that we can appreciate his artistry in our lives, to hone the spiritual skills he is developing in us, his spiritual athletes.

Before we look at how God weaves himself through the experiences of our everyday lives, however, we need to first understand how God reveals himself to all people universally. In Part One we will look at how God makes himself known through means outside ourselves. This is crucial, because we want to make sure we are worshiping the true God and not someone or something that is merely a projection of our own imagination. The principles laid out in the first three chapters are truly foundational to a solid spiritual faith. Without the right foundation, a house will never retain its structure, nor will it last when the hurricanes come. Similarly, your faith needs a solid structure to stand against the storms of life. But once you have a sound understanding of who God is and how he reveals himself outside of subjective experience, you will be equipped to interpret the more subjective side of knowing and enjoying God.

So let's begin the journey that leads to knowing the living, loving, majestic God.

Part One

GOD
REVEALS
HIMSELF
UNIVERSALLY

Chapter One

CREATION: GOD REVEALS HIMSELF TO ALL

Two nights ago there was an ice storm. The next morning when I pulled the shades in our living room to the view of our oaks, shrubs, and evergreens, the scene took my breath away. Encased in their glassy shrouds, everything glistened.

Last night I had noticed how the light from a neighbor's window shone through the glazed tree branches and illuminated the tree. This morning the cherry tree outside our dining room window was a blaze of white light. My four-year-old son, David, asked, "Are there lights in the tree?" It was more beautiful than Christmas.

As the day progressed, the beauty increased. The ice had beaded on the bare branches, and the light shone such that the trees looked as if they were full of stars, stars that had descended from the night to alight in the branches of winter—shimmering and twinkling even through the blaze of the daytime sun. Many of these "stars" twinkled the colors of the rainbow; as I turned my head a little the hues changed from gold and orange and red to violet and green. The sight inspired awe. It stretched my imagination to the point where I could almost believe that sometimes stars do descend and settle briefly in the trees.

Nature is like that. It surprises with a gasp of beauty, it ignites our senses in a blaze of light and glory. It reminds us that we are not the final word or authority, but that an intelligence greater than our own runs the universe, quite apart from our little worlds of problems and cares and stresses.

The Bible, in Romans 1:19–20, says that "what may be known about God is plain to [humankind], because God has made it plain to them. For since the creation of the world God's invisible qualities—his eternal power and divine nature—have been clearly seen, being understood from what has been made, so that men are without excuse." If we do not see, it is because we have chosen not to do so.

METAPHORS OF GOD'S NATURE

Much can be discerned about God from nature. It is his first and most universal revelation to human beings; it is available to all. Yet not all of us have trained ourselves in how to read this book.

Sanna Baker, a poet and children's book author, has developed the art of seeing God in nature. To Sanna, "everything in nature is a metaphor waiting to be unlocked." Everything in nature is more than what it appears; everything points to some truth about God. When I called her today to talk about the light in the ice-encased trees, she said, "I have been trying to think of what the metaphor is here. Maybe it is this: Yesterday the trees were ice-covered, but not as beautiful. It isn't until the sun hits them that the effect is so breathtaking."

Sanna's habit of looking to nature to see God's invisible qualities is deeply ingrained. She grew up in Bemidji, Minnesota, where the skies proclaim the glory of God—amazing sunsets and night skies ablaze with stars, skies that sometimes whisper the mysteries of the Northern Lights. "From earliest times I can remember looking at the star-filled Minnesota nights, having a sense of the immensity of things," she says. "I was taught that God is the Creator of all these things. I was filled with wonder and a sense of awe at who this God must be. Seeing the grandeur of God led me to feel that if the God who created all these things has me in his hand, then I can relax and trust him."

Nature fed Sanna's spiritual life. As a poet, she is particularly attuned to concrete images and metaphors; these speak best to her of God. When she moved from Minnesota to Michigan, and then to Illinois, she went through a period of mourning, of feeling cut off from much of what fed her. But now, she says, she looks for God in small things. God still speaks to her through nature.

Every summer she and her husband, Steve, and three daughters go back to Bemidji for a visit. Last summer, on a Sunday, the family went hiking, way up north in the wilderness. Sanna suggested that everyone keep an eye open to find something that might speak to him or her. That evening they shared what they found. "Interestingly, everyone brought back stones, but each saw something different in them," Sanna says.

Sanna's stones were smooth, beautiful ovals. The smoothness, she learned, was produced by hitting against other hard objects. The metaphor she unlocked: It's the hitting up against hard things that both sharpens and smooths us. "I still have the stones sitting out in my bedroom, where they can be a visual reminder," Sanna says.

Another gift of nature that day for Sanna was the sight of an unusually calm Lake Superior. "As far as I could see was blue, so that it was impossible to see the horizon line. It gave me an image of dying as a sailing out to where life and death meet." These images are special gifts from the Creator at this time in Sanna's life, because she is battling cancer. The stones and the image of death have sustained her faith and helped her fend off questions of "Why me?" Rather than ask that, she rests in the signs of God's continuing care for her.

Through nature Sanna also expresses her own faith. "I planted bulbs yesterday," she told me one Sunday late in November. Immediately I knew that for her, planting was an act of hope.

Not knowing whether she will be around to see the bulbs bloom the following spring, she nevertheless scouted several nurseries to find one that still sold bulbs that late in the season. And she braved the hardening ground to set these bulbs toward life. "Burying these unpromising-looking things in the ground, the freeze that comes after—it seems so unlikely anything will come of them," she says. "Then it's spring, and you have this wonderful beauty and life."

Sanna did see her bulbs bloom. And year after year, they will be a reminder to her family of God's faithfulness and the faith and hope to which Sanna clings.

MAKING ROOM FOR NATURE

My husband grew up in the city—what he calls "the concrete jungle." In contrast to me, a native of New England whose chief pleasure in life was walking in the woods, Gene did not naturally relate to the outdoors. But because he is married to someone who hauls him outside at every opportunity, he has come to appreciate nature more than ever. In fact, he is now almost as avid a bird-watcher as I am, and he finds hiking as renewing an activity as I do. He even enjoys mowing the lawn, because it gives him a chance to be outside. (I can't get him to enjoy gardening, however. Not yet.)

Like many of us, Gene has had to make room for nature in his life. It's so easy to get caught up in our frantic schedules and not take the time to look around us or to renew our souls with God's natural tonic. Phillip Keller, in his book *Outdoor Moments with God*, tells of how one busy, frantic day as he was speeding down the road, he suddenly had the compelling sense that God was urging him to turn off the road and go to the sand pit by the lake. He obeyed, though his outer self enumerated all the things he had to do on that busy, busy day.

He describes what he saw on that spring day: "The whole world was pulsing, vibrant, and energized with new life. Magnificent cumulus clouds climbed into the blue April sky above the mountains. Their glorious reflections adorned the lake in majestic beauty. I stood silent, pensive, waiting, and awestruck by the scene. 'Oh my Father, thank you for such glory, such grandeur!' I inhaled deeply, again and again and again. Peace, His peace, and His presence enfolded me. The rush, the hurry, and the tension of the day ebbed away softly. All was still within." Keller goes on to describe other sights, sounds and smells that renewed him that day, all because he took the time to immerse himself in nature. "This quiet hour's moments had been carved out of a hectic schedule, to remain enshrined in my memory for years to come. All of it was without cost, without money, and without stress or strain."[1]

Isn't that God's way? He delights to surprise us with moments of refreshment, of beauty, of reminders of his presence or glory or power. "Come, all you who are thirsty, come to the waters; and you who have no money, come, buy and eat! Come, buy wine and milk without money and without cost. Why spend money on what is not bread, and your labor on what does not satisfy? Listen, listen to me, and eat what is good, and your soul will delight in the richest of fare. Give ear and come to me; hear me, that your soul may live" (Isaiah 55:1–3a). Note all the references to the senses in these verses: thirst and drinking, eating and tasting, listening and feeling satisfied. God wants to fill our senses with good things. And he delights in doing it in such a way that it is free, not costly. His way satisfies deeply, in contrast to the fleeting satisfaction we too often feel after we manufacture "entertainment" for ourselves.

But we do have to come to him. Though he delights in surprising us with wonderful moments, such as the ice storm or the scene Keller describes, we still have to respond. Keller could have buried the urge to turn off the road and hurried on to meet his frantic day. Many people do. The day the sunlight shone on the ice-covered trees, my friend Charlene Baumbich decided to drop everything and go to the Arboretum. She invited several people to go with her, but all said they had too much to do. "Whatever you have to do will still be there tomorrow," Charlene said. But they didn't go. She did. She went to "listen to the trees," as she put it.

And God did not disappoint her. She spent a wonderful time at a secluded spot she thinks of as her "chapel," listening as the icy trees "talked to one another." She opened a devotional book she had in her car's glove compartment—a book she had not opened in two years. That day's reading was on how important it is to listen to nature! God underscored what she already knew, and assured her that taking those moments for him would not be wasted but forever hallowed.

Perhaps such moments are not only his gift to us, but an opportunity for us to give to God. When he comes to us in nature, our openness is an opportunity to commune with the Creator. I can't help but think that pleases him. Didn't Phillip Keller and Charlene warm God's heart when they took time out from all their busyness to receive God's gift? Theirs truly was a sacrifice of praise—their sacrifice of time for him resulted in a welling up of praise to him for his greatness.

When I took time out the other day to bask in the wonder of the starry trees, he blessed me. I'm sure he made me more productive the rest of the day than if I had turned away from his gift, muttering about how much work I had to do. Instead, I stopped, looked, and drank it all in. That started a wonderful interaction of praise and gratitude to God, blessing from him, more praise to him, until I indeed felt full as from a good meal.

"Here I am! I stand at the door and knock. If anyone hears my voice and opens the door, I will come in and eat with him, and he with me" (Revelation 3:20). Jesus, through whom all things were created and in whom all things are sustained, knocks at the door of our lives through his creation. Let's not turn away when he knocks.

There are so many ways we can invite him into our lives through nature. I encourage you to pick at least one or two of the following things that naturally attract you, and consciously incorporate them into your life. I believe that not only will God speak to you in new ways, but you will warm his heart with your efforts. Looking for his presence, you will find him, and that will sustain you through whatever comes your way.

WAYS TO FEED YOUR SOUL THROUGH NATURE

A hobby that gets you into nature. Gardening is an obvious example. Like Sanna's planting of bulbs, it can be a sacramental activity. Flowers emerging from those shriveled bulbs, a burst of beauty after a long barren winter or a touch of glory in the middle of summer—bulbs are wonderful, as are any flowers. But so are fruit-bearing bushes and vegetables. All attest to a number of things about God: his abundance and imagination (plants can grow from seeds, branches, roots, bulbs), his love of variety (color, shape, form, scent), his abundant provision. I can still remember seeing an apple orchard in Michigan during harvest time. The trees were so laden with red fruit, I could only think of the Garden of Eden. Such abundance!

Tending a garden can be work, but work that brings many sweet and tasty rewards. Author Francine Rivers finds even weeding to be a spiritual tonic: as she weeds, she is reminded of how important it is that she routinely "weed out" the things in her life that keep her from bearing as much fruit as she otherwise could.

Indoor gardening can also be a reminder of spiritual truths. Every winter Sanna Baker plants paper white narcissus bulbs on her kitchen window sill. She does it for more than the pungent bursts of white beauty. They are reminders to her that, no matter how improbable it seems, life returns, a symbol of hope.

Another hobby that can bring you in touch with nature is photography. It is a wonderful way to study the properties of light—itself a rich metaphor, since the Bible says that God is light. Bird-watching, identifying flora and fauna, or collecting things (shells, rocks, leaves, wildflowers) are other hobbies that pull us out of ourselves and force us to pay close attention to the natural world. Hiking, skiing, fishing, camping, sailing, and snorkeling can also enrich the soul.

Plan family vacations that immerse you in nature. Sanna and Steve Baker always made a point of taking family vacations that would enrich their children's sense of wonder. They go up to Minnesota, sail in the ocean, ski in the mountains, or hike in state parks. "I wanted the kids to see things that were real," Sanna says. "Kids get so easily bored." Something that did leave an indelible impression was snorkeling. "The first time I saw those fish, it absolutely knocked my socks off," Sanna says. "We did it at night too, when you could see the phosphorescence." Now, Sanna says, if you offered any of her girls a choice between going to Minnesota or to Disneyland (which they have seen), they would each choose Minnesota. "The real is so much more satisfying."

Sandy and Robert Wright actually crave time in the mountains or on a beach because of how God has used nature in their lives. Their family has been through many wrenching traumas, including stillborn birth, their daughter's open heart surgery, and the death from heart disease of their youngest son, Zachary, at age four. They have noticed that "God has used nature to give us the rest *before* a trial," by settling a deep peace and rest on them that later sustained them when the trial hit. For example, the week before Zach died, the family was snorkeling. Sandy dove down to take underwater pictures of the kids. Zach was totally relaxed, arms outstretched, hands limp as his daddy towed him around. A deep sense that God was giving her a glimpse of Zach soaring to heaven settled over Sandy. Sandy had known all along that Zach would probably die soon. Because of this image, instead of fear, she now felt acceptance and peace.

Sandy says, "The pattern is so clear, that the last time we were in the mountains, Rob and I both noticed a deep rest in our spirits. Turning to Rob, I asked him if he thought something was coming. He laughed and said that if it was, we'd be ready. Sure enough, two 'adopted relatives' passed away within two months of each other, and I discovered I had to face my twenty-third surgery soon."

Sandy and her family were again and again able to find the strength they needed to face such trials because of the unique refreshment they received through creation.

My family always went camping for vacations. Swimming, fishing, catching frogs, scouting out wildflowers, watching for deer and chipmunks, or just sitting and contemplating water from the river slip over rocks—these fed my soul. Gene and I still remember the time we camped at a state park, went on a night hike, and saw an owl, and the time we stayed at a cabin up in northern Wisconsin and saw, for the first time, a bald eagle, a great blue heron, and otters. Memories of vacations spent in nature can become an oasis in the desert of everyday life—a place we can go back to, in our minds, for refreshment. As Sandy Wright said, "Peace, preparation, joy ring in nature, whether it be a beach or a mountain."

Caring for animals, birds, fish, and plants. Breeding dogs or cats, raising orchids, landscaping to cater to wildlife, making a pond in the backyard, or even having a pet can remind us that we are part of God's creation and can open the door to numerous spiritual lessons.

I have always lived with cats. One day I had to take my cat Golda to the veterinarian to have her teeth cleaned. The procedure involved anesthesia, and I had to leave her there for the day. Golda sat in the front seat crying and trembling, even panting in terror. She struggled in my arms when I took her into a room where she would be temporarily caged across from some frantically barking dogs, also caged. How I wished I could make her understand that what I was allowing to happen to her was for her greater good, that I really had things under control, that everything would work out all right in the end! I could not make her understand; she is only a cat. All I could do was talk to her reassuringly, hoping that my presence would make the difference. This incident often comes to mind when I am going through a difficult or scary time that I can't understand. I reflect that no doubt God has a plan, he has promised that he is in control and that whatever I'm going through is for my own good. And as I experience the fear, he is with me, his words there to reassure me.

Establish rituals. These may be daily—a daily walk in early morning or evening, for instance. When I was a child, I had a field I walked to almost every day at sunset. I sat on a little knoll at the top of the hill, looking straight west into the sunset. And there, before I ever really heard the gospel, I felt a sense of God. God used those daily sunsets to keep me close to himself before I ever truly responded to the call of Jesus in my soul.

Missionary Frank Laubach wrote of daily walks up "Signal Hill" behind his house. He describes an encounter with God one such day: "The day had been rich but strenuous, so I climbed 'Signal Hill' back of my house talking and listening to God all the way up, all the way back, all the lovely half hour on the top. And God talked back! . . . Below me lay the rice fields and as I looked across them, I heard my tongue saying aloud, 'Child, just as the rice needs the sunshine every day, and could not grow if it had sun only once a week or one hour a day, so you need me all day of every day. People over all the world are withering because they are open toward God only rarely. Every waking moment is not too much.'"[2] God showed Laubach many more things about himself during those daily walks up the hill and back.

Seasonal rituals can also add meaning and a sense of continuity with nature. Our family picks strawberries in the spring, blueberries in summer, and apples in autumn. For me, it is a way of submitting to the rhythms of nature, reminding me that indeed "there is a time for every purpose under heaven."

Practicing stewardship. Taking care of the earth, whether through recycling, cleaning up an empty lot, renewing the soil of a piece of land, fighting to preserve land locally or keep pollution at bay, volunteering at a wildlife refuge, landscaping your yard to make it nature-friendly—all are ways of participating with God in taking care of his Earth. All can remind us of our own creatureliness, of the intricate balance of nature, and the fragility of our own existence if we do not take care of what God has created.

Studying nature. From the insects in your backyard, to the mysteries of genetics, to the wonders of the galaxy, studying any aspect of nature can open a whole world of God's workings. Physics, botany, zoology, genetics, chemistry, astronomy—any of the natural sciences can cross over into theology. Madeleine L'Engle says that as she studies quantum physics, she gains insights into theology; the concepts in advanced physics point her directly to the mystery and secret workings and great power of God.

We don't have to have a Ph.D. in science to appreciate the order and glory of nature. Simple observation, guided by some field guides or other books, or watching a television program on nature can remind us of God's work and open us to fresh revelation.

What can we expect to learn about God as we begin to invite nature into our lives more? If all nature points to insights into God's invisible nature, what are we to look for?

WHAT CREATION REVEALS

When the Bible talks about God and nature, it usually mentions words like *glory, majesty, strength, power, awesome* (see, for instance, Psalms 29, 65, 104, 147, 148). It also describes the response we are to give: "fear" (in the sense of awe, bowing to his power and dominion); hope; songs of joy; praise. It speaks of the seasons being signs of his faithfulness, of natural signs such as the rainbow as symbols of God's covenant. It uses common natural elements—trees, water, lightning, plants—as symbols for spiritual realities.

Jesus himself opened up how we are to look at creation. In the natural order, we glimpse God's grace as he "causes his sun to rise on the evil and the good, and sends rain on the righteous and the unrighteous" (Matthew 5:45). Jesus told us to "consider"— take a good look at—the birds and the flowers for lessons in God's provision. Many of his parables pointed to nature to illustrate some spiritual lesson: the mustard seed that, though small, grows up to be the largest of garden plants; the grain of wheat that must fall into the ground and die before it can live and produce food; the yeast that works its way through the whole batch of dough; trees that produce good or bad fruit according to their inner state of health. To Jesus, nature was replete with examples of God at work, for those "who have eyes to see and ears to hear."

In nature we experience God through our senses. Through our openness to nature we can sharpen and deepen and educate our senses with what is real, rather than dulling them with what is manufactured and unreal. Nature opens us to a world of plea-sure, joy, mystery, beauty. It awes us with God's power, humbles us with his majesty, dazzles us with his beauty, captivates us with his mystery, inspires us to trust in his providence, fills us with joy with his extravagance.

Meditating on God as Creator reorients us by stilling our questions with a glimpse into a larger perspective. Job's questions about the nature of suffering died on his lips after God's series of questions about how he, God, runs his creation (Job 32:3–6). As Sanna Baker told me, "There is this sense that if the God of all this has me in his hands, everything will be all right."

Being open to God in creation means taking the risk of "reading into" certain natural phenomena. Lois Carr, who with her husband Robert and family served as a missionary to Uganda for several years, talks about the special place rainbows came to occupy in her life. Rainbows of all kinds seemed more plentiful there. "I saw pale-shaded rainbows, so large that only a portion of the arc was visible high in the sky, and mini-rainbows, where the whole arc was contained in a small valley between two hills. Sev-eral times we viewed double bows side by side, with one slightly brighter than its twin," she wrote in a newsletter to supporters.

On their last day in Uganda, God used this natural sign to reassure her of his presence. It was hard to leave Uganda. Lois felt physically, emotionally, and spiritually exhausted. As she drove her vehicle up the neighbor's driveway, which ran beside her tall bamboo-like fence, she paused at the main road before pulling out and looked for on-coming cars. Her eyes were drawn to the gate of her property, and she and her children gasped. "There, only a few yards from us, was a rainbow that rested at the foot of the now-locked gate and then arched over the road and finally faded into the trees of the house across the road.

"'Wow! It's so close!' said one of the children. 'It's a sign of God's promise that he'll always take care of our house!' offered another."

To Lois, the picture of this rainbow was a vivid reminder of God's presence at a time when he felt distant. "I had been instantly filled with hope—to think that God still had not abandoned me, that he loved me, was pleased with me, and knew my future!"

Was Lois reading too much into that rainbow? I don't think so. Not only did God place the rainbow there, but the Holy Spirit helped her to interpret the sign. She says, "I guess the Lord knew that on *that* particular day, I needed a visible reminder of his grace and mercy toward me. Now, as we see God's work through the . . . Ugandans, I have assurance that his promise, just like that rainbow, extends to them as well."[3]

We are to be open to such signs from God, such encouragements. He may choose nature as his usual vehicle for revelation to you, as he does with Sanna, or only occasionally, as he did with Lois. But he will speak, he will reveal, if we are willing to receive. Too often we go around blind to God's billboards—nature.

But some things we can't learn about God from nature. Nature points us to God. But to get the right messages, to interpret the signs rightly, we need more. Nature alone can lead us astray, causing us to worship the creation rather than the Creator behind it. Or we can be confused, because nature isn't all beauty and light.

Annie Dillard, in *Pilgrim at Tinker Creek*, tells of watching a frog being sucked to nothing before her very eyes by a giant water bug. This beetle injects a poison into its victim, a poison that dissolves all the victim's insides, and then sucks it dry. Other carnivorous animals devour their prey alive. "We don't know what's going on here," Dillard says, as we witness "power and beauty, grace tangled with violence" in nature. "It could be that God has not absconded [from creation] but spread, as our vision and understanding of the universe have spread, to a fabric of spirit and sense so grand and subtle, so powerful in a new way, that we can only feel blindly of its hem."[4]

To enlarge our vision, to give us a true language in which to speak of God, we need further revelation. We need something that appeals not just to our senses, but to our minds.

We need the Word of God.

Chapter Two

THE WORD: GOD REVEALS HIMSELF TO THE MIND

People today are searching. Oprah Winfrey earnestly urged people to open up to God, whatever their concept of God might be. The Twelve-Step program of Alcoholics Anonymous and the other Anonymous groups urge people to turn their lives over to God, as they understand him. One man I know insisted, "I believe in God, Jesus, whatever you want to call him." People are getting the idea that God is whatever we want to make him (or her) to be.

I am skeptical whenever I hear someone talk about "what God is like." I am skeptical because I think the human heart would rather make up its own god, a god we feel comfortable with, rather than bow to the authority of the God who revealed himself in the Bible.

The very first commandment in the Ten Commandments is, "I am the Lord your God, who brought you up out of Egypt, out of the land of slavery. You shall have no other gods before me. You shall not make for yourself an idol in any form. . . ." (Exodus 20:2–4a). Yet even as God was giving the commandments and the law to Moses on Mount Sinai, Aaron and the people were down below making a golden calf and calling it God! How quickly the Israelites fell into idolatry, despite having witnessed great miracles of God's power in Egypt, the miraculous deliverance by parting the Red Sea, and miraculous provision of food in the form of manna and quail. (See Exodus 3–16, 32.) It seems a very ingrained part of the sin impulse to make for ourselves gods we can control, gods we can understand, rather than submit to the true God who made heaven and earth and has absolute moral authority over our lives. Idolatry—setting up false gods—is the sin human beings find hardest to shake—perhaps because we truly are spiritual beings, and we have to worship something.

GOD ON HIS OWN TERMS

God exists on his own terms, or he wouldn't be God. He would be projections of our own longings, our own imagination, our own needs.

If God wants to be known, it makes sense that he would have attempted to make himself known. And indeed he has. All religions have their Scriptures, but there is something unique about the Judeo-Christian Bible made up of the Old and New Testaments. These Scriptures claim that God worked in history, through a people (the Jews) he chose to reveal himself to and through. After revealing himself to an entire people, he narrowed down his revelation to one Man, one Jew, Jesus Christ, who is God incarnate, the Word made flesh, the final revelation of God.

To anyone who seriously wants to know God, the necessary starting point is the Bible. It reveals God as he wants to be known, God as he revealed himself in time and space. The Bible is, and must be, the final authority for all other "revelations" from God. If you believe God is telling you something, but it contradicts a principle or truth in the Bible, you are being misled. The Bible is meant to comfort, guide, instruct, encourage, inspire. Its wisdom has been tested for centuries. Here is truth, and more than mere wisdom: Here is the revealing of God to humankind.

Not that we can ever fully comprehend the Bible. It is too vast, too complicated. And to be quite honest, some of it is confusing, some of it appears to contradict itself, some of it is obscure. But I have found this to be true: If one begins to accept it as the revelation of God, and begins to live by it, a whole new world opens up. "In your light we see light," says David in Psalm 36:9. The Bible is the measuring stick, the final authority, the sun that defines what light is. Without the Bible, we wouldn't know how to "find" God through other things—nature, other people, our everyday lives. The Bible tells us what to look for.

Accept the Bible as revelation, as truth to be followed, and you will find a rich banquet of spiritual food. (If you want to know how the Bible can enrich your life, I recommend to you Psalm 119. It is the longest Psalm, and is essentially a love poem about God's words. Whenever I find my Bible study to become a little dry, I go back and read Psalm 119 to get re-inspired.)

Perhaps your problem is that you just haven't been able to understand the Bible. Or your Bible reading has grown wearisome and dull. Perhaps you haven't yet seen how it can be relevant to your life. How can the truths and stories written so long ago shed any light on contemporary problems such as how to raise children, or spend money, or choose a career?

Actually, I have found God's Word to be amazingly relevant on these topics and more. The more I read of it, the more I absorb, the more I begin to think along biblical lines, the easier it is to discern God's answers to very contemporary questions.

Let me give you an example of what I mean.

DEALING WITH THE ENEMY

I had the unfortunate experience of being threatened with a lawsuit. Needless to say it was distressing. I, who never had any enemies before, was suddenly the target of an enemy's attacks.

It has been my practice these last few years to read through the One Year Bible, which has daily readings from an Old Testament passage, a New Testament passage, a Psalm and a couple of Proverbs. As soon as I found out about the lawsuit, it seemed every day's readings for several weeks had at least one reference to enemies. Also, my pastor preached a wonderful sermon from 2 Kings 6:8–23, "God Has the Enemy Surrounded." It was uncanny how much comfort and guidance I received directly from God's Word. Comfort that God was in control. Guidance about what to do and what not to do: "A man of knowledge uses words with restraint, and a man of understanding is even-tempered. Even a fool is thought wise if he keeps silent, and discerning if he holds his tongue" (Proverbs 17:27–28). Psalm 143 became a perfect expression of my thoughts, feelings, fears, and desires regarding the situation. And following the New Testament instructions to love my enemy and pray for him led to a surprising peace.

In a time of contemporary trial, the ancient words of the Bible were God's vehicle of direction and strength. Truly it is God's Word to me, illumined by the Holy Spirit, which is at work in my life. And so it is meant to be, for all our lives.

THE LANGUAGE OF GOD IS BIBLICAL LANGUAGE

If we are to learn the language of God, then, we must first learn the Bible. God's particular language to each of us will never contradict the language of his larger revelation. The Bible is like my mother tongue, which is English. If I think God is speaking to me in a foreign language, I can be sure it's not God who is speaking.

The Bible is like the form of a sonnet, very strict: exactly fourteen lines, a precise rhyming scheme, and iambic pentameter rhythm. Within these parameters, there is freedom to say anything you want. But if you create a poem with sixteen lines, you no longer have a sonnet.

So it is that God reveals himself solely within the context of Scripture. Add something he hasn't revealed, strategically leave out some crucial truth (such as saying that Jesus was not divine or not human, or didn't really rise bodily from the dead), and you no longer have an accurate picture of God; you have an idol of your own making. Yet within the context of biblical revelation, there is almost limitless opportunity to learn of a limitless God.

LET THE WORD DWELL RICHLY IN YOU

The challenge becomes, letting "the word of Christ dwell richly" in you (Colossians 3:16). Here is where our individuality begins to make a difference in how we approach the Scriptures.

I have long been fascinated by the complexity and uniqueness of each human being. Our minds and bodies are infinitely complex, and like snowflakes, no two people are ever alike. The Psalmist David wrote long ago, "I am fearfully and wonderfully made," and he praised God for his handiwork (Psalm 139:14). Part of what it means to be complex and unique is that we each have different ways we take in and process information.

In his book *Frames of Mind*, Harvard psychologist Howard Gardner proposes that there are at least seven kinds of "intelligence": logical-mathematical, musical, bodily-kinesthetic, linguistic, spatial, interpersonal and intrapersonal. Every normal person possesses each kind of intelligence to some degree, according to Gardner. Most of us have a few fairly well-developed intelligences, some that are about average, and some that have caused us problems. Our strongest are what we would normally call our natural strengths. A person's intelligences seem to be "hard-wired" according to genetics, but environmental and cultural pressures will enable someone to develop or neglect the development of his or her native intelligences. Thomas Armstrong has picked up on Gardner's ideas and applied them to the field of education. According to Armstrong, each of us has a unique learning style based on our combination of intelligences.

In studying Gardner's and Armstrong's theories, it occurs to me that our approach to learning the language of God will also be connected to the way he has created us, that is, to the intelligences he has "wired" into us. As I read through the Scriptures each year, I am struck by the variety in Scripture: history, story, poetry, drama, pathos, logic, prophecy, law, proverbs and aphorisms, letters, biography, and more. The multiple styles and forms serve not only to get the point across, but also to convey what God wants us to know about him in ways that the human race, with its spectrum of individual and cultural contexts, can understand and receive.

Each of us has a particular learning style, based on our particular set of intelligences. I believe an understanding of one's particular learning style can revolutionize one's approach to Scripture, both to what is studied and how it is studied. Some of us will be attracted to the historical books first and foremost, others to the poetry or the expository letters. Some will learn best through hearing, some through retelling or teaching, some through journaling, some through singing. Once you have a handle on how you best learn, you can begin to devise your own Bible study plan that takes into account the most natural way for you to take in information and make it yours.

Let's look at the various "intelligences" and how they might be incorporated into a study of the Bible.

SEVEN COMPONENTS OF A LEARNING STYLE

Keep in mind that all of us are intelligent in each of the following areas. As you read through the descriptions, think about which of them strike a chord in you, which sound most like you. Your particular combination will point to your individual learning style.[1]

Linguistic intelligence. If you're strong in linguistic intelligence, you probably have highly developed auditory skills and are attuned to sound. You will have a natural attraction to words, whether in verse, lyrics, puns, jokes, or names. You may especially enjoy writing, reading, telling stories, doing crossword puzzles and/or playing word games like Scrabble. You learn best by verbalizing, hearing, or seeing words.

Spatial intelligence. This is the intelligence of the artist, mechanic, inventor, architect, engineer. Those strong in this intelligence think visually, in images and pictures. When using spatial intelligence, you are aware of your surroundings, where things are and how they look. Drawing, designing things, building, and simply imagining are all functions of spatial intelligence.

Logical-mathematical intelligence. If people with a strong tendency for the linguistic think in words, and the spatially gifted think in pictures, the logical-mathematically intelligent think conceptually. They are interested in patterns, categories, and relationships. They love to experiment with the environment to discover "What will happen if?" If you love brain teasers, logical puzzles, and games of strategy such as chess, you are probably strong in this intelligence. You may enjoy computers and science, accounting, engineering, or perhaps even philosophy.

Musical intelligence. If you have musical intelligence, you probably already know it. You're likely to play a musical instrument or sing in a choir. At the very least, music is important to you, and is an integral part of your life: You often listen to music or have it on in the background, you enjoy attending concerts, you can easily remember melodies, and music often tends to run through your mind. You are also likely to be tuned in to nonverbal sounds in your environment—birds chirping, the noise of traffic, a distant bark of a dog—sounds others might not even notice.

Bodily-kinesthetic intelligence. Michael Jordan's genius on the basketball court is a graphic picture of this kind of intelligence in action. Always on the go, people with this strength process information through their bodies. This intelligence may be expressed through involvement in sports, theater, mime, dance, or in fine-motor coordination needed for sewing, crafts, typing, drawing, and fixing things. Sometimes children with this intelligence are labeled as "hyperactive" because they are always moving or fidgeting.

Interpersonal intelligence. Those with this intelligence are "—people smart." They have a natural ability to understand, communicate, and organize others. If you are able to tune in to other people's feelings and motives, if you tend to know what's going on in the lives of the people around you, chances are you excel in this intelligence. You will learn best by relating to and cooperating with others.

Intrapersonal intelligence. This intelligence involves an ability to tune in to one's inner world, to feelings, perceptions, dreams, ideas, and intuitions. If this is your strength, you may feel a strong need for solitude and have goals and dreams that propel you on a path that may set you apart from many of your peers. Whatever you do, it has to be meaningful in some way to yourself and, preferably, to others as well. This is the intelligence we use when we attempt to relate directly to God, when we are trying to sense his presence directly.

In a way it is very artificial to segregate these intelligences, as Gardner points out. But it is a useful way of thinking about what I have elsewhere called "energized abilities."[2] And because these intelligences are integrally related to how we learn, they are relevant to thinking through how we can best take in truth about God, especially through the Scriptures.

BIBLE STUDY YOUR WAY

Ever since I committed myself to following God's way, I have recognized the importance of studying the Bible, and I have learned various methods for doing so. I went through an in-depth curriculum from InterVarsity Christian Fellowship called Bible and Life, which taught me how to study the Bible inductively. I attended Bible studies. I used Bible study guides and devotionals. And, as I mentioned, I began using a system of reading through the Bible every year.

Often I felt that I was straining—Bible study became simply a duty. It was only when I started studying about learning styles and experimenting with different approaches to Scripture that God's Word became alive to me in new ways.

Discovering that I am linguistic, intrapersonal, interpersonal and musical, in that order, has helped me understand why I love the narrative, poetic, and mystical parts of Scripture best. Majoring on studying these portions of Scripture has been very enriching. I do not neglect the history, or the epistles, but for my private devotional time I find it most enriching to focus on those parts of Scripture that seem to speak to me in a very special way.

Because of my particular learning style, I take in Scripture best through the written word, through hearing words (in sermons), through meditating on a Scripture passage and interacting with it in a journal. Because of my interpersonal bent, group Bible studies also enrich me. And music seems to reach the parts of my soul that are beyond words.

Someone whose learning style is made up of spatial, bodily-kinesthetic and logical-mathematical intelligences will need a far different approach. Let's look at which biblical books a person with each strength might find most attractive, and some of the ways one can approach Bible study accordingly.

Linguistic. Since the Bible is mostly words, a linguistic approach is the most natural. Like me, those who are linguistically inclined may find the narrative and poetic parts of the Bible most compelling. They probably pay close attention to sermons, and get a lot out of them. They may enjoy listening to the Bible being read on tape, and may profit from memorizing the Word. They may find appealing Bible study guides that use an inductive approach—where a Bible passage is explored for its principles and applied to life. Books about the Bible are also likely to attract the linguistic learner.

Spatial. Spatial learners think and learn visually and in pictures, and may be most affected by the vivid pictorial language of the Psalms and books of prophecy, as well as by Proverbs and Ecclesiastes with their vivid word-pictures. Spatial learners might also want to concentrate on biblical narrative, such as is found in the Gospels and Old Testament books such as Genesis, Exodus, Esther and some of the Old Testament historical books (Joshua, Judges). If this is your style, a good Bible dictionary, guide, or atlas that includes maps and flow charts of the history will help you picture what is going on. You might want to draw pictures of Bible stories that are particularly meaningful (or puzzling), or give your own visual spin to verses through calligraphy. Artist Timothy Botts is a marvelous example of this; he uses color and shape and form and size in his calligraphic expressions of Bible verses and passages. But you don't have to be a Tim Botts to make use of a spatial talent; the important thing is to express and use the gift you've been given to enrich your intake of God's truth.

Musical. Musical learners probably love the Psalms the best, which were, after all, originally songs. Musical learners can set Scripture to song and so "hide it away in their hearts," to paraphrase the psalmist. I find it interesting that when Paul exhorted the Colossians to "let the word of Christ dwell richly" in them, he went on to mention singing: "Let the word of Christ dwell in you richly as you teach and admonish one another with all wisdom, and as you sing psalms, hymns and spiritual songs with gratitude in your hearts to God" (Colossians 3:16). Listening to, singing and even making up psalms, hymns and spiritual songs will be an integral part of the learning and worship of the musical learner.

Bodily-kinesthetic. Our culture does not value this ability, except in its worship of sports. In many other cultures, physical skills such as balance, dexterity, strength, and endurance are both valued and developed. Yet Scripture itself is full of references to bodily sensations: "Be merciful to me, Lord, for I am faint; O Lord, heal me, for my bones are in agony. . . . My eyes grow weak with sorrow. . . ." (Psalm 6:2, 7) "I am poured out like water, and all my bones are out of joint. My heart has turned to wax; it has melted away within me. My strength is dried up like a potsherd, and my tongue sticks to the roof of my mouth. . . ." (Psalm 22: 14–15) Besides the Psalms, Job, Ecclesiastes, the Song of Solomon and Proverbs all contain vivid bodily language, and hint at a mindset that is far more tied to the senses than we have become accustomed to in our culture.

Bodily-kinesthetic learners usually need to process information through bodily movement. This can make it difficult to sit through sermons in church on Sunday! It may help to take notes when listening to a sermon; in this way you are involving the body to some degree anyway. You might also try reading Scripture while riding a stationary bicycle, or walking around the neighborhood as you recite memorized verses. If you're also linguistic to some extent, you may find it helpful to walk or jog or somehow move while listening to the Bible being read on tape. You might re-enact Bible stories dramatically, or through dance. One young friend of mine choreographs dance sequences that correspond to certain biblical stories or themes. Not only does this help her incorporate Scripture into her own life, but it enriches those of us who watch her dance by adding a new dimension to our experience of the Word.

Logical-mathematical. Every time I read the book of Romans, I am struck by the fact that Paul the Apostle was gifted in this area. Probably others who are "logic smart" find Paul's Epistles especially helpful, and there is much to be gained from a study in doctrine (which is theological logic).

If you're strong in logic, you will also appreciate and benefit from systematic study of the Bible, whether a word or topical or book study, and will want to have access to a good Bible dictionary, study Bible, and commentaries. You might even try computer programs that help you study the Bible. (I have an electronic study Bible—a parallel cross-referenced edition featuring the King James Version, New International Version, and Nave's Topical Bible. It is still in the box. Can you tell the relative strength of this intelligence for me?)

Interpersonal. Since people with this intelligence learn best through interacting with others, group Bible study is ideal. I don't think there's anything wrong with making group study the main way one takes in the Bible, provided it's a regular part of one's life. Teaching the Bible, whether as a group Bible study leader or in some other setting (such as Sunday school), is also very helpful for interpersonal learners. Another possibility would be to go through a study guide with a spouse or close friend. The key for this learner is the interaction with other people. Interpersonal learners also probably get a lot out of listening to preachers, teachers, and the like, though it's usually the face-to-face encounters that mean the most. Studying the life of Jesus and other biblical characters may be especially meaningful for interpersonal learners.

Intrapersonal. For those whose strength is intrapersonal—the ability to look within—meditation on Scripture in solitude is truly spiritual food. Such learners do not take a remote, academic approach to the Bible; what they crave is a personal encounter with God, an intimacy with him that is felt as well as known intellectually. Such people may seem a bit "mystical" to others, but it is a necessary part of their approach. Solitude is important to everyone, but crucial to the intrapersonal learner because only in solitude can he or she become still enough to sense the presence of God.

In Western Christianity, the tradition that supports this approach is called the contemplative tradition. Coming from an evangelical tradition myself, I found it necessary to read people like Richard Foster and James Bryan Smith for suggestions on how to foster this kind of growth.[3] I particularly like Smith's suggestions for meditating on a verse of Scripture with an attitude of openness to what God is saying to me personally.

Journaling is also a useful tool for many people who are intrapersonally intelligent, especially for those who are also linguistic and/or spatial. (A journal doesn't have to contain words; it can be pictures as well.) Elizabeth Canham, in *Journaling with Jeremiah*, models a process of keeping a journal while studying the prophetic book of Jeremiah. This biblical book of prophecy is itself something of a journal of Jeremiah's struggles with God, the nation and himself. Books of the Bible that especially speak to intrapersonal learners are those that answer the essential questions of human existence, such as "Who am I?" and "Why am I here?": Genesis, Job, the Psalms, Ecclesiastes, Isaiah, Jeremiah, the Gospels, Romans, Colossians and Revelation.

OPEN MIND, OPEN HEART, OPEN BOOK

I have suggested some ways to approach and enrich your study of God's revelation of himself through his Word. I encourage you to try different things, and keep track of which approaches lead to the Word coming alive for you.

Remember, God does want to speak to you, personally and truly. Learning to listen to his Word is the first and foundational step. It is a step you will continue to come back to, again and again, for it is what your whole life with God is built upon. But necessary as it is, reading and studying the Word of God is not the end. It is possible, after all, to misunderstand, misinterpret, or otherwise get Scripture out of balance. Even when we think God is "saying something" to us through the Bible, we often need to test it. The classic, and humorous, example of the way the Bible can be misused is the story of the man who, longing to hear "a word from God," opened his Bible at random. The book opened to Matthew 27:5: "Judas went away and hanged himself." Feeling shaken, the man tried again. This time his finger fell on Luke 10:37: "Jesus told him, 'Go and do likewise'"!

The corrective to wrong interpretation and understanding of Scripture is the body of believers. In the next chapter we will see some of the ways God comes to us through his current body on earth, the body of believers known as the church.

Chapter Three

THE CHURCH: GOD REVEALS HIMSELF HUMANLY

Today I felt blocked. Growing increasingly fearful of not making my deadline, I fell prey to fear. Fear was like a huge felled tree, blocking my path. I could not see over or beyond the tree, and I didn't know how to climb over it without getting bruised. I was at a standstill.

Now, I have learned that when I'm at a standstill, the best thing to do is act. But not randomly. The first tiny step toward the tree was prayer. "Dear Lord, please speak to me. Please help me. What do I do?"

My Day-timer already had the plan: Read a certain book today, among other things. But God's small, quiet voice seemed to say this: "Set aside all your books now. It's time to write. Write anything. Just start writing."

But still I felt blocked. The tree remained, solid as an oak. I simply could not write.

So I took the next step: I picked up the phone and called Charlene, a dear friend. Charlene is not only a fellow writer, she is someone who seems to be specially placed in my life by God to be a mirror. Charlene will reflect back who I am, good points and bad, in such a way that I can somehow receive it. She is one of God's special mirrors of truth in my life. I don't always like what she has to say. But somehow, God's grace coats her words and they go down easily enough for me to really hear.

She and God did not fail me this day either. I poured out what was blocking me, I described my tree. "I can't seem to write my God book," I told her. "I mean, who am I to think that I can write a book about knowing and hearing the voice of God?"

Charlene said, "I want you to hear what you are saying, every word. 'My God book.'"

I didn't understand. She explained. "This is your book, your life, your experience of the living God. He is giving you the thoughts and the words. This book is not being written by some academic, but by a real, laughing, struggling, weeping, dancing child of God whom God talks to in many different ways. There are people out there who need to hear what you—YOU—have to say. And it's just Satan's voice—and ego—that is trying to convince you that you don't have anything to say."

She went on. "I have heard the passion you have about this book. God wants to communicate something through you. And it's just ego—a false humility—that is trying to get you to think otherwise." Ego. Ouch.

The more we talked, the more I heard her—and myself—remind me of things I already knew. I just needed to hear it—again, and not for the last time, I'm sure—from the mouth of another.

Her words also confirmed what God had been whispering to my soul—about myself, about the work he set before me, about his faithfulness. And about what I should and should not do that day. "Forget the reading," Charlene said. "You need to be writing. Today." Word for word, almost exactly what I felt God had told me earlier that morning.

Hearing those words from my friend gave me strength to believe that I do know my Shepherd's voice. That when I next hear it, I will be able to trust it without seeking confirmation from another source.

On the other hand, God wants us to seek him through other people. This idea of a cozy little personal relationship with God, minus the community of other believers, is nowhere in the Bible. Not in the Old Testament, where God spoke to his people collectively, and not in the New Testament. Yes, Jesus dealt with individuals. But he chose twelve to become close to him, to learn from him *together*. And Paul and the other epistle authors never imagined their letters would be read in private by individuals. Their letters were sent to churches, to groups of believers, and they addressed issues that not only individuals but the congregations needed to understand. To be Christian is to be called into community.

And it means God will speak through community. He, the relational God, often chooses to speak to us through our relationships.

THE RICHEST REVELATION OF ALL

God revealed himself to our senses through creation and to our minds through his Word, as we have seen. But his greatest revelation is through taking on human nature. In his love for human beings, he himself took on human flesh. In Jesus Christ he gave us "God with skin on." Jesus was God's final and best, his most glorious revelation. The writer of Hebrews says, "In the past God spoke to our forefathers through the prophets at many times and in various ways, but in these last days he has spoken to us by his Son, whom he appointed heir of all things, and through whom he made the universe. The Son is the radiance of God's glory and the exact representation of his being, sustaining all things by his powerful word" (Hebrews 1:1–3a).

As we look at Jesus in the Gospels, we see God in action in human affairs. We see the perfect, sinless God-man taking on human sin, dying in the place of sinners, and rising to triumphantly conquer death. We learn, especially through the Epistles, what it means to put our faith in the life, death and resurrection of Jesus Christ and thus, somehow appropriate his life into our own. These truths are mysterious, and glorious.

But there is another, just as mysterious and glorious. And that is that Jesus Christ is still present on this earth, in bodily form. When Jesus ascended into heaven to sit at the right hand of God, he sent his Holy Spirit to indwell all those who believe in him and seek to walk in his ways. Those believers, past and present, comprise the church, which the Bible calls the body of Christ. As the Holy Spirit indwells each believer, the life of Christ is lived out in the world. "There is one body and . . . one Lord . . . speaking the truth in love, we will in all things grow up into him who is the Head, that is, Christ. From him the whole body, joined and held together by every supporting ligament, grows and builds itself up in love, as each part does its work" (Ephesians 4:15, 16).

We in the Western world have been so individualized that we often miss this truth. Or we have a very superficial experience of Christ coming to us through other people. But Jesus always intended us to find God through—and in a sense, be God to—other people.

Jesus said that following him would mean dying to self—to our instinct to put our own needs and agenda first—and living for others. But as we do that, we bring Jesus to others: "The man who loves his life will lose it, while the man who hates his life in this world will keep it for eternal life. Whoever serves me must follow me; and where I am, my servant also will be" (John 12:25, 26).

My family experienced God's practical care through others before the birth of my second child. Since my son, David, had been premature, when I experienced regular contractions seven weeks before my due date in this pregnancy, I called the doctor right away. It took nine days in the hospital under various medications to stop the labor enough for me to go home. Then I was on bed rest and medication at home for another couple of weeks.

During those three weeks, other people stepped in to provide meals, run errands, and take care of my son. Friends provided encouragement through calls and visits. But what probably meant the most was that they prayed.

The very first day in the hospital, I called Charlene and told her where I was, asking her to pray. Shortly after we hung up the phone, she called back. She told me, "I prayed after we hung up, and I had this very clear image in my mind, Diane, of a perfect rose unfolding. I had this sense that it had to do with birth, and that this baby will be perfect." Charlene added, "I don't usually get visions or images, you know, but this time it was so strong." I felt a reassurance in my heart when she told me that. That night, two dear friends, spiritual parents from my college days, came through town and visited me in the hospital. They brought with them a gorgeous, fragrant rose. I put it in water. In the following days, the sight and scent of that rose tangibly reminded me of Charlene's image, and the fact that others were praying for the baby and for me as well.

When my daughter was born only a week before the due date, she was just like that perfect rose I had been given. We named her Christine Rose. Her middle name will always remind us of the prayers and encouragement of God's people—the care he took for her and us even before she was born. Without those prayers and the tangible help I was given, who knows if she would have been the full-term, healthy baby she was.

God made us such that we need him more than we need food and water, and we need each other almost as much. Jesus is the Bread of Life, the living water that will quench our deepest thirst. The Apostle John narrowed the essence of the spiritual life down to two things: "This is his command: to believe in the name of his Son, Jesus Christ, and to love one another as he commanded us" (1 John 3:23).

The life we experience as we walk with God is a shared life: "the life of God in the world does not have its meaning in isolated units, but in a fellowship of those who share their life in him," writes Rueben Welch.[1] We show our love for God as we show practical love for each other: "This is how we know what love is: Jesus Christ laid down his life for us. And we ought to lay down our lives for our brothers" (1 John 3:16).

Part of God's grand design is that we need "God with skin on" to fully know who God is and what he is like. God began that revelation through the incarnation of his Son, Jesus Christ. God continues that revelation through the lives of his people. We need other believers in order to fully know and love God.

HOW DOES GOD REVEAL HIMSELF THROUGH PEOPLE?

To answer this, we need to ask another question: Why do we need other people at all?

We need each other because we are human, and Jesus Christ, the human God, is no longer bodily with us. (Even if he were, he would be limited by time and space. As it is, through the Holy Spirit he has overcome those barriers.) We human beings have physical, emotional, mental and spiritual needs that can often be met only by contact with another human. When I faced writer's block, I believe God was trying to guide me out of it. I heard his voice. But somehow I couldn't act until I heard the same message coming from the lips of another human being. We just aren't always spiritual enough to trust our spiritual intuitions without confirmation from the physical, outer world—which often means, from people.

Then, too, God made us with those needs and cares about them. He promises to meet our needs, but usually chooses to do so through other Christians—those who believe in him and are walking in his light. That is why he commands us, again and again, to love. And he defines that love in 1 John 4 as meeting the needs of other people, and having our needs met through other people.

When Grace's marriage broke up because of her mentally ill husband, she was emotionally and financially devastated. For several months there was no income at all. A strong believer, Grace prayed that God would take care of her and her three children. She received a call from her church: "For the next three months, you are to shop at a certain grocery store, and the bill will be taken care of." Another time, when the real estate taxes were due, a friend slipped something into her pocket and said, "I don't want you to look at this until I leave. And then promise me you'll use it." It was a check for $1,000. Overwhelmed, Grace called her friend back and tried to protest. How could she accept such a gift? Her friend said, "Look, you pray for God to meet your needs. What do you expect him to do? Drop it from the sky? *This* is how he meets your needs. I'm not struggling right now; you are. The money means nothing to me."

Grace's friend was right. In God's economy, one person's overflow is often meant to meet another person's needs (2 Corinthians 8:14). This kind of giving and receiving is more than a simple transaction; it is a powerful witness to both giver and receiver of how God supplies our tangible needs. Many single parents I know attest to the fact that God became especially real to them when other people helped them with very practical, physical needs.

The unemployed people I interviewed for my book, *Men in Search of Work and the Women Who Love Them,* shared that they experienced God's care when other people spontaneously offered to help with job leads, college tuition, or brought over food or took the children out shopping for clothing. God promises to provide for our temporal needs. But that can only happen through the caring of other people. When we experience such caring, our faith in God's promises is bolstered.

MIRRORS OF OURSELVES

Another reason we need each other is because we rarely see ourselves, let alone others or God, as we really are. We need others to hold up a mirror to ourselves.

Sometimes we need others to point out our gifts. Our truest gifts are those that come so naturally and easily to us that we don't even recognize them. Not until someone else points out, "You really know how to draw people out" or "Most people aren't as organized as you are," does that talent come into focus for us.

Other times we get caught in a trap of self-deception. We need someone who can lovingly show us our problem and remind us of the truth.

Sometimes we need people to love us when we can't love ourselves, to forgive us when we can't forgive ourselves. We need others to mirror not only who we are, but to speak God's truth into our reality.

This kind of mirroring happens only in close relationships. It happens in families, for better or worse. Husbands and wives can bring out the best and the worst in each other; parents can nurture a child's potential or crush it.

It can happen in close friendships with others who are committed to both us and the truth. When we experience these kinds of relationships, we do well to pay attention. God will speak to us when we are in relationships where there is a commitment to "speak the truth in love" (Ephesians 4:15).

It takes courage to lovingly confront another person about his or her sin, and it takes humility to receive correction from another. We tend to go to the extremes—either harshly pointing out someone's failures in the heat of anger or hurt, or avoiding conflict altogether. But in several places the Bible tells us and shows us that a loving rebuke is life-giving. When Nathan the prophet confronted David with his sin, David repented and wrote a beautiful psalm that stands as a testimony of repentance and forgiveness (Psalm 51). Jesus gave us the perfect balance when he told us to make sure we take the log out of our own eye before we try to remove the speck from our brother's eye. But notice, we *are* to try to remove the speck in our brother's eye. It doesn't belong there. We need each other to take the specks out of our eyes (and to realize we have logs in our own).

Once I had occasion to hold up a mirror to a friend who had wronged me. I spent much time in prayer beforehand: I had to examine my own motives and confess my own sins. I prayed for the right timing and the right attitude on my part. The time came, and I gently told her how I felt she had wronged me, and how it affected me. To her credit, my friend did not become defensive, but really listened. She faced her sin, explained her own struggles, and asked for prayer. We both reaffirmed our friendship and commitment to each other's spiritual growth. It was a difficult but healing experience for both of us. Our friendship remained intact. Indeed, the confrontation was probably the only way we could have stayed friends. The experience helped her to face some painful truths about herself, and she grew tremendously from the process of facing, confessing, and seeking help for this particular struggle.

MANY GLIMPSES OF GOD

Another big reason we need other people is that none of us has the whole picture of God. He is too vast for any of us to comprehend completely. I suspect we will spend eternity exploring the vastness and beauty of God's nature. In this life, God reveals various aspects of himself to each of us. As David Hazard points out, "What we know of God is what he chooses to show us of himself. And he has reasons for letting each one of us know some certain aspects of himself but not all of them."[2]

One of those reasons, I think, is to connect us to other believers. I need to know your God, and you need to know mine. If I am struggling to believe that God truly will provide for my needs, I need your experience of God as Provider to bolster my faith. If you cannot forgive yourself for some past sin, you need my experience of God's forgiveness to strengthen your ability to accept forgiveness.

A friend of mine lost her pregnant daughter in a tragic car accident. It was the greatest challenge her faith had ever faced. It was the witnesses, she says, those people who had suffered grief and kept on believing, that kept her steady during the months of grief that followed. One person in particular did a weekly spiritual checkup with her. Other believers who knew her well "really *took care of me* during those months," she says. Someone from her church wrote a beautiful poem about her daughter and gave it to her. My friend asked a talented artist to make it a calligraphy art piece, which is for her a comforting treasure. It is a memento of God's tender care through other believers during a time of great grief. As they suffered with her, she experienced something of the One who bears her sorrows and carries her griefs.

We need each other because the God you have come to know may be just the part of God I need to see. We each are limited by our own personalities, preferences, gifts and experiences. My friend who lost her daughter and grandchild needed to know, from people who had experienced it, that God was indeed "the God of all comfort." When Gene was unemployed, I clung to other people's stories of how God provided for their needs. Their experience bolstered my faith in "Jehovah-jireh," the God who Provides, until I too had my cache of stories of how God provided for us. Now it is my responsibility to share my experiences of God with others. And so the circle ripples out. A new brick is laid in the building God is trying to construct on earth.

The God you know is part of your spiritual gift to the world. Because I do not have the whole picture, I cannot afford to ignore your concept of God. I am to take it with discernment, yes, always holding it up to the light of Scripture. But if you see God as "the God who expects us to work out our faith in society," I need to listen. Perhaps God will use you to stir me out of my complacency to some form of social action. If you see God as a God who desires our intimate friendship, perhaps God will use that to introduce new directions in my own prayer life.

LEARNING TO LISTEN TO GOD . . . THROUGH OTHERS

If God truly does reveal himself through other believers, and we truly want to know God better, it makes sense to seek God through our relationships. Here are some practical suggestions for how to nurture relationships God can use.

Observe godly people. Several people serve as "role models" to me. Some are part of a small group that has been together for years. As I have watched these godly women and men raise their children and deal with all kinds of tragedies, from the death of a parent or a child to battles with cancer, I have seen God at work. Their faith, rubbing against my own, has strengthened mine. Their lives have shown me new approaches to parenting, to being a wife, to facing hard times . . . to following Christ.

Observing godly people can also mean reading biographies and the works of great Christians. Some of the people who have deeply affected my life and work are no longer living—Amy Carmichael, C. S. Lewis, Søren Kirkegaard, John Calvin, Frank Laubach, Corrie Ten Boom. Other, more contemporary influences on my life and work—Madeleine L'Engle, Richard Foster, Gordon MacDonald, Richard Bolles, J. I. Packer, John Stott—I know mainly through their books. God has used their thoughts to influence my own.

Hebrews talks about being surrounded by a great cloud of witnesses. I thought of that when someone told me of how important the first-century witnesses were to her during a time when she began to seriously doubt Christ's resurrection. She read, prayed, studied, and talked with a friend. In the end, it was the witnesses that convinced her. "All those first-century Christians who were there, who had everything to lose by believing such a tale. And they believed and taught it anyway, even died for that belief," she said. Godly witnesses are potent sources of knowing God.

Pay attention to "God's mouthpieces." In my life God uses a handful of people in a special way. I call them "God's mouthpieces to me." They may be "kindred spirits," or very different from me. God uses each type in a different way. The "kindred spirits"— those who seem to see life in the same way I do—offer validation and support and encouragement. Those who are very different from me help me to see parts of myself and of reality that I wouldn't naturally see. They hold up a mirror to my blind spots, showing me myself as I really am, but in a way that somehow I can receive it. God uses both kinds of people.

Some of his mouthpieces can also be considered mentors. Mentors are those who have gone on before us in some area. Sometimes a mentor is someone in similar life experiences, but who has already been through some of what you are going through now. Sometimes it's someone who has honed the same gifts you have, and can show you the way.

Such mentors are usually older than we are, or at least further along in some life stage. They can be alive or dead. Author Michael Phillips, who has updated and edited George MacDonald's works, talks about how important George MacDonald was to him, spiritually, personally, and professionally. George MacDonald lived in a different century, yet his works touched something deep within Michael. Spiritually, MacDonald showed him a deeper way of knowing God as Father. Personally, his example helped Michael hang on to his faith through some difficult trials. And professionally, MacDonald's writing showed Michael the power of fiction to illustrate spiritual truth, which helped spawn Michael's own successful writing career.

Some people find it helpful to begin a structured relationship with one or more persons who can become "God's mouthpiece." It may be an individual, as with a prayer partner or "spiritual director," or a group. I am encouraged by the number of small groups that are springing up, especially among men, that emphasize deepening trust and accountability to others.

We need to put ourselves into a position where God can speak to us through other people. Depending on your personality, you may want a more structured or a more casual approach to opening yourself up to other believers. The point is to take time to nurture relationships with those people, dead and alive, whom God can use or has used in some special way.

One of my regrets is that I let lapse a relationship with a woman who reached out to me in my early twenties. God used this older woman to enlarge my understanding of him, of creativity, of what it means to serve and to endure. But sadly, I let the relationship die when I moved to another town. Some relationships are meant to die a natural death, but I don't think that was one of them. I let one of the fires God used to warm me go out, simply by lack of attention.

Ask questions—and listen. I've noticed that people are often willing to talk about how God is working in their lives—if I take the time to ask them. Often such discussions come up in a Bible study group. Or in personal conversation with someone I know well. Sharing my own struggles often opens the door. This level of sharing happens when I ask, in discussing someone's situation, "Where do you perceive God in all of this?" The question often provokes the other person to focus on the positive, and usually he or she has something to share that opens both of our eyes to new truths about God.

My friend Hope, a single mother of two school-age children, accepted a job offer and moved her family from Illinois to Seattle. Five months later, she was unceremoniously told that the job would be discontinued. Because it had been such a struggle to get established in a new community, Hope decided to return to Illinois. We got together and prayed for her various needs: for housing, for a job for her, for her own sense of God's presence. As we focused on where God was in all that had happened, many positive things came into focus: Accepting that job had forced her to move on professionally—and now God was providing a whole new career direction, one that suits her very well and pays her adequately. The Seattle job had paid her well, and she had bought a good computer—which is now indispensable for her home-based business. Taking the job and making the move had shown her and the children new depths of resilience and capabilities in themselves. As Hope focused on where she saw God's hand in her life, my own vision of God expanded. I too felt encouraged that God could and would use some of the difficult experiences in my life for good, just as he had with Hope.

Serve others. As we pour out our gifts to enrich the lives of other people, we glimpse God—in them and in ourselves.

When Gene's struggle with employment was over, I wanted to put it behind me and move on. It had been a difficult period for both of us. But I heard too many stories, saw too many statistics, of people in similar pain. When Gene and I went through it,

there seemed to be no acknowledgment anywhere of the problem, and that deepened the pain. So I decided to write a book to
help others learn what we learned the hard way. In doing so, I had
to revisit the pain. I didn't want to. But as I talked with other
people in similar situations as part of my research, I learned many
things about God. My view of how God provides was expanded.
My view of God himself and his purposes changed: I realized that
he is less concerned about our personal comfort than that we help
other people in their need. Through the testimony of others, I saw
how "when God takes everything else away, he gives us himself,"
as one man put it. And I saw from my own experience how God
can take something difficult, like Gene's and my experience, and
turn it into something full of purpose and healing.

Let others see how God is working in your life. Sharing our
experiences of God deepens those experiences for us, as well as
others. Sanna Baker found in her illness a whole new way to serve
other people. "People who wouldn't have felt comfortable
approaching me with their doubts and fears before have now
been coming to me," she says. As they came and Sanna shared her
life and faith, her own view of how God can redeem hard situations was deepened. As people asked her about her faith, that
faith was clarified, for Sanna as well as others.

Be open to how God works in others. One marvelous way to do
this is to pray for people. After I had prayed for weeks with a single mom for good child care, I was filled with joy to see how God
provided. Praying for people raises our expectations that God will
act, and sensitizes us to look for answers. Sometimes we're even
part of the answer, as when someone expresses a need and we realize we have the resources to meet that need. Then it's a wonderful
feeling to know that God is using us as his instruments of blessing.

Pay special attention to those closest to you—your spouse,
parents, children. Sometimes it's hardest to believe God will
change those we know best. We're so aware of their failures, and
too often we ourselves try in vain to change them. I've been learning, with my family, that the best way is to ask God to change

them, and then look for evidences of his work. My biggest thrill and glimpse of God's character has been when I have given up trying to change someone and prayed instead, and then seen those changes unfold naturally and beautifully.

Explore what other believers have discovered in the past. If we limit our view of God to what we can discover through our contemporaries, we will be poor indeed. Remember, none of us has the whole picture of God. We need the insights of believers from other eras and religious points of views. One wonderful resource for "tasting" some of the great Christian thinkers of the past is *Devotional Classics* by James Bryan Smith. Reading Augustine, Pascal, John of the Cross, Teresa of Ávila and others has opened me up to new ways to view God. Their views often lead me to probe the depth of my own spirituality, and expose the superficiality of my own era. For instance, rarely do I find in contemporary authors as great a concern about pride as I do in the "classic" spiritual writers. Yet the Bible is full of God's hatred of pride. I need believers of other eras to show me the blind spots of my own age. I may not agree with much of what I read. That's okay. What is important, I believe, is that I wrestle with it, before God, asking him if there is anything here he wants me to know.

It can be a tricky balance. We need to be open to other people's answers about God, contemporary or not, but also discerning. Their way may not be right for us—or not right for us *now*. There is a difference between appreciating what others know of God and how they express their faith, and following that for ourselves. I can appreciate someone's approach to very structured prayer or Bible study, and acknowledge that it works for them. But my way may need to be more open and unstructured. For me, that is how I best express my faith and open myself up to God.

To experience God, we need to become students of nature, of the Word, of his work through his people, past and present. But even within these general revelations, different chords are struck in different people. Someone may see God clearly in nature and need to feed himself regularly at that source. But someone else may feel they can take or leave the out-of-doors. Is the second person less spiritual? Not necessarily. So much is a matter of who we are and where we came from, for God meets us at those points and takes us where *he* wants us to go. Our business is to follow him.

And the exciting part of it all is that he forges a unique path with each one of us, one that has never been followed before and never will be followed again. That is what we will explore in the coming chapters—how to discern and map out your own truly personal relationship with the living God.

Part Two

God
Reveals
Himself
Individually

Chapter Four

GOD SPEAKS PERSONALLY

Other parents have told me that "everything is easier with the second child; you know what to expect." While I understand what they mean—I am less nervous with this my new baby—I also find the statement a bit misleading. I am finding that this new person, only seven weeks old, has her own particular set of needs and preferences. In many ways I'm starting over afresh, getting to know her.

With my son, David, I could never distinguish between his cries. Christine's "I'm hungry" cry is a "la-la"; her "I'm tired" cry is a fussy "eh-eh"; and her cry for attention is a rather imperious "ah-ah." I'm learning that she cries when she is falling asleep or in light sleep. Like my son, David, she seems to hate being alone; she wants to be held most of the time. She loves to take a bath. Learning to "read" this new little person is like learning a whole new dialect of a language I once thought I understood.

Taking my turn in the church nursery underlines for me this sense that from birth, each person is one of a kind. One child will only go to sleep if she's held and rocked; another won't sleep unless he's put down and left alone. This toddler cries for mom the whole time; that one is off to explore every nook and cranny, hardly noticing when the parent left. I'm convinced we come "wired" from birth with a great deal of our personality.

Personality theories that seek to "type" people are helpful to some extent, and I find them fascinating. But in the end, even similar personality "types" are each unique. Nobody can be categorized or fit into a box. That is why a personal relationship with God means that God speaks to each of us uniquely.

I tested this theory out by conducting an informal survey of a couple of dozen people's experiences of how God communicates with them. I also found out their personality type, and looked for similarities in each type's experiences. Sure enough, there were similarities among similar types. But each person's experience also stood out as unique. God seems not to like to repeat himself exactly very often.

I see that also wherever I look in creation. Not only do species vary wildly from each other, there is great variety within species. Because I enjoy watching birds, I have a feeder right outside my kitchen window. In the spring and fall, we get birds at our feeder I never see any other time—birds with beautiful shadings of red or green or yellow. I run to my bird book to identify them, only to face frustration: none of the pictures in the book looks exactly like what I see outside my window. I guess; I'm not sure if I'm seeing pine grosbeaks or purple finches or house finches. My conclusion is that even within species, no two individuals are exactly alike. Oak trees may all have rough bark and three-lobed leaves, but the shape of each tree is different from any other.

GOD'S REVELATION: THEN AND NOW

God loves variety, revels in individuality. We see it in his creation; we also see it in the Bible. The people God called to serve him came from all sorts of backgrounds and had all sorts of personalities. Abraham was apparently very wealthy; God called him out of his comforts to become a wandering nomad. Joseph was torn from his family, made a slave, and thrown into prison, yet eventually became second to the king himself. The prophet Isaiah was an adviser to the kings of Judah; Micah, who prophesied during the same period as Isaiah, was a country boy. Daniel came from a prominent family but was dragged off to Babylon and served in a foreign government. In the New Testament, we see Jesus choosing disciples with different personalities and from different social and economic spheres: fishermen, a tax collector, a political zealot. God takes us as we are, and molds us into what he wants us to be.

Scripture shows that God also reveals himself through a great variety of means. It's not always clear how God spoke. What is clear is that whatever the means, the person knew when it was God speaking. Throughout the Old Testament, we see God coming to people in dreams, visions, nature, words and, perhaps, inner impressions of words. Does God still speak in such ways today?

Yes and no. In biblical days, each time God communicated, it was to reveal something new about himself or his plans to his people. Since the birth, life, death, resurrection, and ascension of Jesus Christ, and the completion of the canon of the New Testament, there is no further, "new" revelation from God. Hebrews 1:1–3 says clearly, "In the past God spoke to our forefathers through the prophets at many times and in various ways, but in these last days he has spoken to us by his Son, whom he appointed heir of all things, and through whom he made the universe. The Son is the radiance of God's glory and the exact representation of his being, sustaining all things by his powerful word. After he had provided purification for sins, he sat down at the right hand of the Majesty in heaven."

New revelation of who God is has ended, because it reached its fullness and completion in Jesus Christ.

However, *illumination* is ongoing; that is, God's work in applying the already-revealed truths to our everyday lives, in very real, practical, and personal ways. In fact, it is the main role of the Holy Spirit to bring to life what Jesus Christ revealed and apply it personally to each one of us (John 14:26).

In this sense, God does still speak today. And I believe he still uses a variety of means to do so. He will not speak new revelations. Beware anyone or anything that claims to be "a new revelation of

God," of anything that does not square with Scripture! As I stressed in chapter two, God's language is always a biblical language. He will speak revealed truths into our individual personalities, circumstances, relationships, problems and desires. As he does so, it will be as if we receive a personalized love letter every day from him. That letter will always be written in the same language, that is, the Bible's language.

Once we learn the basics of this language—what God wants to say in general—the Holy Spirit will begin to help us recognize what God is saying to us in particular. He will help us see God's hand in every aspect of our daily lives. In this way, God will become as real and personal to us as he seemed to the people with whom he spoke and walked in biblical times. In fact, Jesus told his disciples that they would actually be better off, be closer to him, once he came to them through the Holy Spirit.

But before we can recognize God at work in our daily lives, we need to know the kinds of things to look for. What does God want us to know about him? What will the Holy Spirit be teaching us day by day?

What God Wants Us to Know

Who he is. God wants us to understand what he's like, his character and attributes. He wants us to get a sense of his majesty, his wisdom, his grace, his mercy, his wrath and judgment of sin, his goodness. He wants us to know that he is truth, he is love, he is holy, he is the Way. He wants us to know him by his many names and titles: Elohim, the Creator; El Elyon, God Most High; El Roi, the God who sees; El Shaddai, God Almighty; Adonai, the Lord; Jehovah, the self-existent One; Jehovah-jireh, the Lord will provide; Jehovah-rapha, the God who heals; Jehovah-nissi, the Lord is my banner; Jehovah-mekoddishkem, the God who sanctifies you; Jehovah-shalom, the God of peace; Jehovah-sabaoth, the Lord of hosts; Jehovah-raah, the Good Shepherd; Jehovah-tsidkenu, the Lord is my righteousness.

One of the richest studies I have done is to study these names of God as revealed throughout the Scriptures, along with key images for God (rock, shepherd, Father, counselor, etc.).[1] The more I steeped myself in God's attributes as described in the Bible, the more I saw those attributes reflected in nature, in the lives of other people, in the circumstances and challenges of my own life.

I study nature and learn more about Elohim's faithfulness, majesty and wisdom, his love of variety and beauty, his attention to detail in creation. I pray for some material need and find it supplied by another believer, but behind that person's generosity I glimpse the hand of Jehovah-jireh providing for me. I trust God to protect me from an undeserved attack and experience firsthand the truth that God is my defender, my banner.

God wants us to know, love and adore him for who he is. Every name, every attribute, is fathomless. The more we seek to know and love God, the more he will reveal himself to us.

God wants us to know who we are. We can't know ourselves fully until we know God, for it is only in relationship to God that we can be who we are meant to be. God, the Creator who knit each one of us together in the womb, is the only One who truly knows us through and through. He knows who we are, who we've been, who we can be. He, the source of all life and anything good, means us to have life in all its fullness (see John 10:10).

The good news that God made us for a relationship with him bumps into some bad news: a big part of our nature is bent away from, not toward, God. God is pure holiness, and each one of us falls short of his standard. "No one living is righteous before you," declares Psalm 143:2. The best we can do is not good enough: "All of us have become like one who is unclean, and all our righteous acts are like filthy rags; we all shrivel up like a leaf, and like the wind our sins sweep us away" (Isaiah 64:6). In short, "all have sinned and fallen short of the glory of God" (Romans 3:23). The Holy Spirit brings this fact to full force, while at the same time revealing Jesus, the answer to this dilemma (John 16:8–11).

Once we come to Christ as our Savior, and ask him to change our hearts, this revealing of who we are takes on a new quality. God begins to show us not only who we have been and who we are now, but who we can be. "If anyone is in Christ, he is a new creation; the old has gone, the new has come!" Paul exults in 2 Corinthians 5:17. Elsewhere, Paul also says, quoting Jeremiah 9:24, "No eye has seen, no ear has heard, no mind has conceived what God has prepared for those who love him." Then he adds, "But God has revealed it to us by his Spirit" (1 Corinthians 2:9–10).

We can expect God to show us, by his Holy Spirit, who we are and who we are becoming, in Christ. Since I came to God in my teens, I can honestly say that God has shown me as much about myself—my sin, my weaknesses, and something of my strengths—as he has shown me about himself. What he does is reveal who he is in the context of who I am at any given moment. He never shows me who I am without also helping me understand who he is in that context. So, when I fall into some of my old hurtful patterns, God patiently opens my eyes so I can see my sin clearly (sometimes it takes awhile, to be honest). Then he reminds me who he is and what he has done about my sin. When I ask for forgiveness, he restores my joy (though not always right away).

God also kindly reveals my strengths and opportunities to serve him through exercising them. This is true self-esteem, to know I am loved deeply by a great God, and to know that he has given me gifts that can be part of his greater purposes. I have seen him use events, even painful events from my past, for good purposes in the present, and thus I see more of his goodness and sovereign ability to transform bad into good. He has used deep needs to force me to cast myself on him and trust his goodness and care. The more I learn about myself, no matter what it is—my sin, my needs, my gifts, my uniqueness—the more I end up seeing of God. Not because I am godly, of course, but because he is there at every turn.

Another reason God wants us to know ourselves is to better understand our individual path to him. The goal for each of us is to know and love God. But each of us has a unique way of finding God and expressing our devotion. I am learning that the more I understand of myself, the better I am able to receive and appreciate what God has for me. I touched upon this in chapter two, in discussing different methods of Bible study. Understanding that images and scriptural narratives are most powerful for me, I have focused on word studies in my Bible study. Knowing that I best process my experiences by writing them down, I keep a journal to track my spiritual journey. These methods may not help others, but they work for me. Knowing myself in these ways has helped me find my own best path to spiritual growth. Trying different approaches to Bible study and devotions and paying attention to which methods work best for you will set you on your own path to growth. I believe that God wants us to learn about ourselves, if that learning is done to widen our capacity to know and love him.

God wants us to know how he feels about us. God has emotions; he feels for us. The Psalms and the books of prophecy are full of emotion, both human and divine. He is jealous, wanting all the love of his people. He gets angry with us when we sin. He also delights in us. One of my favorite Bible verses is found in the little prophecy book of Zephaniah: "He [God] will take great delight in you, he will quiet you with his love, he will rejoice over you with singing" (3:17). God sings over us!

He also weeps over us. Jesus wept over Jerusalem because he longed for them to know him. We can grieve the Holy Spirit, Scripture says. It's sobering to know that when I speak harshly to my child, or disobey God's clear direction, that he actually hurts over my behavior. My words, thoughts, and actions can pierce his heart just as surely as my own child can pierce mine. When I remind myself that God actually feels something when I disobey him, I am pushed into the realm of relationship rather than following a set of rules. And that makes all the difference in my own response: I want to confess. I want to change. I want to please, not hurt, the God who loves me.

God wants us to know that he has a plan for us, good plans: "'For I know the plans I have for you,' declares the LORD, 'plans to prosper you and not to harm you, plans to give you hope and a future'" (Jeremiah 29:11). He wants us to know that he forgives us: "If we confess our sins, he is faithful and just and will forgive us our sins and purify us from all unrighteousness" (1 John 1:9). Most of all, he wants us to know that he is our heavenly Father who loves us, who longs to call us his children: "How great is the love the Father has lavished on us, that we should be called children of God! And that is what we are!" (1 John 3:1)

This is the essence of the whole Bible: God communicating to our hearts how much he loves us. He doesn't want us to know it as an intellectual fact, either; he wants us to *feel* loved, to know in our experience that we are deeply loved. "God has poured out his love into our hearts by the Holy Spirit, whom he has given to us" (Romans 5:5).

One of my favorite passages is Ephesians 3:14–20, in which Paul prays for the Ephesian congregation. Here's what he prays: "For this reason I kneel before the Father, from whom his whole family in heaven and on earth derives its name. I pray that out of his glorious riches he may strengthen you with power through his Spirit in your inner being, so that Christ may dwell in your hearts through faith. And I pray that you, being rooted and established in love, may have power, together with all the saints, to grasp how wide and long and high and deep is the love of Christ, and to know this love that surpasses knowledge—that you may be filled to the measure of all the fullness of God."

Wow! Here's what strikes me about this passage: First of all, all relationships have their foundation in God, who is supremely relational. Second, his Spirit works with power in our inner being, where he enables Christ to dwell in our hearts through faith. We can believe that Christ is actually living within us, we can tune in to him in our inner being, by the power of the Holy Spirit. Third, that the Spirit roots and establishes us in love, and he gives us the spiritual power to "grasp" this love—to hold it as our own, to know and feel deep within, without a doubt, that God loves us beyond measure. Finally, to know this love is to be "filled to the measure of all the fullness of God."

The more we experience God's love, the more godly we will be. Most of us have this the other way around: We think that the holier we are, the more we will feel loved by God. But God's love always comes first; it is what motivates obedience. In John 17:6–26, Jesus prays his great prayer for his followers, just before he is arrested. He says that he made God known to his followers, and will continue to do so, "in order that the love you have for me may be in them, and I myself may be in them." Eternal life is to know God, especially to know the love of God that is all wrapped up in his great plan of salvation.

So, God breaks into human lives to show us his great love for us. God continues to break into individual lives in a myriad of ways to convince us of his steadfast lovingkindness.

But God has two other things he wants us to know.

God wants us to know his purpose. God desires us to know his purpose, not only for each of us as individuals, but for history as a whole. The Bible reveals that he took great care, and many centuries, to accomplish his elaborate plan. First, he calls out a nation to whom he reveals himself. He works in the history of that nation, Israel, to show them who he is and who they are. Then he narrows his focus to one person, Jesus Christ, from this chosen nation. Through Jesus' life, death, resurrection and ascension, God accomplishes his salvation. Then he branches out again, living through the Holy Spirit in his people, who are to spread the news of God's desires for his creation throughout the world. And someday, Scripture promises, Christ will come again to judge sin with finality and usher in his new kingdom fully.

This is the big picture. Within this, each of us has a part. God works everything together in our individual lives both for our good and for his larger purpose, which is to be conformed to the likeness of Jesus (Romans 8:28–29). To understand that God has a larger purpose than our immediate happiness is essential to a life of trust and openness to his work in our lives.

God doesn't always reveal the specifics of his purpose to us in our everyday lives, but he often graciously reminds us of the *fact* that there is a larger purpose. This in itself often brings great comfort, the comfort of restored perspective. Especially when circumstances are very dark, we can implore him to remind us of his greater purposes.

God wants us to know how we can serve him. Relationships, if they are healthy, are two way. When we grasp God's love, we are moved to love him back. How do we do that? Through serving and obeying him. And he delights when we do so. Therefore, I believe one of the things he longs to show us is how we can respond to him in service. This too will take on its own unique aspects, as we'll see in chapter ten. So often we agonize over what God's will is. But when we believe that he wants to guide us, that in fact he calls himself our Guide and promises to make the way clear, we can begin to rest in that promise and look for ways he's fulfilling it as we go about our daily business.

A TRULY PERSONAL RELATIONSHIP

God will speak these truths into our individual personalities, circumstances, relationships, problems and desires. And he will do it with such great respect for the uniqueness he has created in each of us, that if we pay attention, we may begin to discern a unique means, a unique "language" that seems to reach us best. Let me give you an example.

Some psychologists have noted that in childhood we learn how to determine when we are loved. We learn from our family and from significant others outside the family what it means to love. "After learning different things about expressing love, we begin to write our own definition or 'language' of love, and it becomes an integral part of our personality. We have chosen one or more means of communication that we will value, accept and use as indications of love."[2] Some actions that have been identified as "love languages" in human relationships are: meeting material needs, helping each other, spending time together, meeting emotional needs, saying it with words, touch, being on the same side, bringing out the best.[3]

If it is true of human relationships that we are specially attuned to certain ways of receiving the message, "I love you," isn't it also true in our relationship with God? Because of our own needs and experiences, we are shaped to receive the message of God's love in unique ways. Because God is truly a loving, merciful Father who "knows our frame," he comes to us in terms of our own "love language." He really wants us to get the message!

All of the above means of showing human love are also used by God. He is the Lord who provides, meeting our material needs. He is our helper. We spend time with him in prayer and reading the Word, and he communes with us. He heals and meets our emotional needs, and through prayer is always available to listen. Through his Word he tells us over and over how much he loves us. Through his people he often touches us when we need "God with skin on." He is our Advocate, the one who is on our side when enemies or our own conscience condemns us. And, because we are a new creation, he is dedicated to bringing out the best in us, redeeming our past and transforming it into a beautiful future.

God reveals his love and purpose for us in terms we can understand emotionally and experientially. A relationship with the God of the Bible is truly a personal, unique relationship. Just as each human relationship is unique, based on the personalities and shared history of the persons involved, so our relationship with God is unique and develops a history of its own. The Holy Spirit is God's presence in our *daily lives*, and I believe we are meant to know his presence and friendship and see his hand amid the ordinariness of life. As we do so, we grow deeper in love with him, and the relationship deepens. As we see his gracious hand in our lives, we realize, we *experience* that we are loved. "This is love: not that we loved God, but that he loved us and sent his Son as an atoning sacrifice for our sins" (1 John 4:10). "We know that we live in him and he in us, because he has given us of his Spirit" (1 John 1:13).

When we really grasp that God loves us, saves us from all that would rob us of life, we become new people. A motivation to be holy, as he is holy, is born. New love for people takes hold of us and grows into a life-giving tree bearing fruit for others to enjoy.

But it all begins, I submit, with falling in love with the living God. And that happens when we consciously open our eyes to God at work in our lives. He is at work, you know. Every second, every day, in every way. Too often we miss it because we haven't learned to open our eyes, to *listen*. It always struck me that Jesus often ended his parables and teachings with the words, "He who has an ear, let him hear." In the book of Revelation, as Christ reveals his special word to each of the seven churches, he repeats the same phrase, "He who has an ear, let him hear what the Spirit says to the churches."

Just as Christ searched the hearts and character of each of the seven churches and had a special word for them, so he does to us.

How do we "develop an ear" for what God is saying to us individually? We begin by understanding what to expect him to say, as we've seen. The next step is to look for ways God has spoken to us in the past, so we can discover more of his ways with us as individuals. Then we must learn what our attitude should be so we can hear, and not filter out, God's continuing messages to us.

Chapter Five

TRACING YOUR
SPIRITUAL AUTOBIOGRAPHY

I know a musician named Jack. He teaches music at a large university on the West Coast and is involved in many kinds of music making, including leading a church choir. He feels God has called him to be a musician, and he seeks to serve God through his music.

One of Jack's delights for a decade was conducting the university orchestra. But after several years he began to grow uneasy because his various responsibilities left him little time for his greatest love, performing as a violinist. He began to wonder about his priorities and re-evaluate the gifts God had given him.

One day, unexpectedly, a former member of the orchestra appeared on his doorstep. The student and Jack visited, and the student shared wonderful things about how much Jack had helped him in his musical career. When the student left, Jack felt as if he had received a special gift in that student's encouragement. As he went to his office, he reflected on the letters he had also received that very week from former students who had written to thank him for his input into their lives. He entered his office feeling good about his work.

That's when he saw the letter. The letter unexpectedly and summarily dismissing him from his position as conductor of the orchestra. Stunned, Jack drove to the beach to walk, pray, and try to sort out the implications of this news. On the way, he turned on the car radio. The music that was playing was the very first piece he had conducted with the orchestra years ago. Jack switched off the radio; he couldn't listen to it.

The following week Jack was scheduled to leave for vacation. He talked to his boss about his dismissal, then went home. As he got in the car to leave for vacation with his family, he again turned on the radio. This time the music he heard was the *last* piece he had done with the orchestra.

To Jack, the whole experience had been framed by real and symbolic manifestations of God's care and communication. How else could he explain the "coincidence" of those two musical works being programmed by a radio station at those critical moments? Why had those supportive students chosen to act at those specific times? These events worked together to convey a message: "This was a whole, and now it has achieved its completion." There was a symmetry to the events much like that of a musical form: an introduction, a beginning, a middle, and ending. It was as if God had designed this experience specifically to communicate to a musician. For Jack there was a sense of closure wrapped in God's love and secure plan, and this allowed him to rest in the rightness of things even in the midst of the pain of change.

As it turned out, leaving the orchestra did allow Jack time to perform more. He looks back on this benchmark experience as evidence of God's personal love and guidance. It is an anchor of belief he can hold on to even when the way is not quite so clear.

GOD'S CREATIVITY IN OUR LIVES

Jack's experience beautifully illustrates what Luci Shaw once observed about her own life: "God is as creative in how he breaks into our lives as he is in the original creation." God the Creator encountered Jack as a musician—not just in this instance, but other times as well. In this way, God not only confirmed his love, but did so in such an intensely personal way that Jack is still deeply moved every time he thinks of it. The *means* of this encounter with God in terms of music said to Jack, "I love you intensely. I love *you*, Jack, in all you are. The gifts I have given you are blessed, and I honor them."

Never forget that God *wants* to communicate with us. He wants us to encounter him in such a way that our relationship is ever rekindled. Revelation 3:20 is often used in terms of evangelism: God standing at the door of an unbeliever's life and knocking. But the context is really the church. Christ is speaking to the church in Laodicea, a church that was lukewarm, neither hot nor cold toward him, a church that thought it had everything it needed but didn't know it was "wretched, pitiful, poor, blind and naked." To this church Christ said, "Here I am! I stand at the door and knock. If anyone hears my voice and opens the door, I will come in and eat with him, and he with me." This wonderful invitation is for anyone who lacks spiritual passion, but who is willing to find and seek more of God.

Other biblical images describe how God woos us. God is always the one taking the initiative. "We love, because he first loved us" (1 John 4:19). While we were still sinners, helpless in our sins, Christ died for us in that ungodly state (Romans 5:8). Sometimes we respond by turning toward him—or away. Most often we are simply deaf. Hosea 11 describes how he woos us and tries to nurture us, and we either don't recognize it (verse 3: "It was I who taught Ephraim to walk, taking them by the arms; but they did not realize it was I who healed them."), or we turn away to depend on lesser gods (verse 5).

THE IMPORTANCE OF REMEMBERING

The heart of the matter is our relationship with God. The greatest commandment is to love God with all our heart, mind, soul, and strength. God wants us to know him, to love him, to participate in what he is doing in his world. He wants us to perceive what he is doing so that we can take a greater part in his big plan. When we see him at work, we learn more of him. When we get to know him better, we can respond to him in obedience.

If we examine our relationship with God from the beginning, when we first became aware of who he is, to the present, we will find hills and valleys of faith and doubt, obedience and disobedience. But if we search specifically for "God's footprints," we will all find times when we have encountered God in a special way. He is always at work, in the world and in our lives. To see how he is working is to rekindle our faith and obedience.

To train ourselves to see what he's doing now, it's helpful to first look back at what he's already done. This practice has biblical precedence. Throughout the Old Testament, God tells his people again and again to "remember ... remember ... remember":

We're to remember his work in our lives: "Remember that you were slaves in Egypt and that the Lord your God brought you out of there with a mighty hand and an outstretched arm" (Deuteronomy 5:15).

When we're fearful in the present, we're to remember how he helped us in the past: "Do not be afraid ... remember well what the Lord your God did to Pharaoh and to all Egypt" (Deuteronomy 7:18).

We're to remember our own disobedience and failures, for they too are part of our relationship: "Remember this and never forget how you provoked the Lord your God to anger in the desert" (Deuteronomy 9:7). Why? I think it's so that we see God's hand of discipline in the right perspective. Also, because it shows us his grace, even in our disobedience. Psalm 106:7–8 says, "They did not remember your many kindnesses, and they rebelled by the sea, the Red Sea. Yet he saved them for his name's sake, to make his mighty power known."

We're to remember and be encouraged by the wonderful things he has done, not only in biblical history but in our own personal histories: "Remember the wonders he has done, his miracles, and the judgments he pronounced" (1 Chronicles 16:12 and Psalm 105:5).

When God seems absent, we are to remember when he was present: "Remember the Lord in a distant land, and think on Jerusalem," God tells Jeremiah and the people who were captives in Babylon (Jeremiah 51:50).

TRACING GOD'S PATH MARKS

Though God is always doing a new thing, he also has been working in your life in certain ways. When you look back on your life in the process I will describe, you will begin to see your life in a new way. You will notice patterns and discern a bigger picture. You will begin to perceive God's hand in the events, relationships, decisions, and Scriptures that add up to a pattern. In a sense, what we are doing is like a child's activity of "connecting the dots." The "dots" are the individual experiences of God's work in your life. When you identify and begin to "connect" them, a "picture" emerges, a pattern of what God has been doing in your life thus far. This picture will bolster your faith, reignite your sense of God's love and involvement with you, and define further directions and possibilities for service.

To look at the ways God has tried to break into your life and how you have responded, I offer some suggested exercises. Each of these is designed to help you stand back and pinpoint the specifics of how God has worked in your life thus far. We have seen that he can speak through nature, through the Bible, through other people. Now we want to focus on your life—what specific means has he used, and how did you respond?

Take your time with these exercises. Add to them step by step, piece by piece, as ideas come to you. You'll notice I have added a number of different techniques and approaches that will appeal to different kinds of people. Start with whatever approach strikes you as most interesting, and don't be afraid to experiment. Again, you are unique, and that uniqueness will work itself out even in the way you approach constructing your spiritual autobiography.

CONSTRUCTING YOUR SPIRITUAL AUTOBIOGRAPHY

The purpose of a spiritual autobiography is to construct a picture of your relationship with God—how it started and has continued to the present. As Moses recited the history of the Israelites in Deuteronomy, and as Joshua set up stones as a perpetual memorial reminding the people forever of how God enabled the Israelites to cross the Jordan, so you will construct a tangible record of your relationship with God.

We'll look at your personal "grace points," starting with *experiences* that somehow seemed like direct experiences of God's grace and working in your life. Experiences that had a spiritual impact on you. Experiences where something happened that only God could have orchestrated.

With each experience or incident we will explore its *spiritual significance*, what *image of God* you formed, and your *response*. Any of these four things may be positive or negative. For instance, one of my experiences was studying Eastern religions before I became a Christian. The significance was that it deepened my spiritual thirst. The image of God as an impersonal force was negative (that is, unbiblical), but it led to a positive response: It fed my search for a more personal God.

Once you've recorded your experiences, we will look for patterns to discern a particular "love language" you and the Lord have developed in your relationship.

PREPARATION

Pray. Before beginning, take time to pray. Ask the Holy Spirit to guide this time, to bring thoughts and memories to mind that come from him. James 1:5 says, "If any of you lacks wisdom, he should ask God, who gives generously to all without finding fault, and it will be given to him." God wants us to remember how he has worked in our past. When you ask him to show you these things, you can be sure he will answer.

Get quiet and private. Make a time commitment of 15 to 30 minutes to start off with. Decide how often you want to have a session—once a day, once or twice a week, once a month.

Look through the following six suggestions and decide how you want to approach this gleaning of ideas stage. Different approaches work best for different people. Here are some possibilities:

1. Jot down short phrases as they come to you, randomly or in outline form.

2. Use a technique called "clustering," which helps the free flow of ideas. I use this all the time when I want to access ideas quickly. The non-linear approach helps one tap into the part of the brain where images and feelings dwell, and tends to open up a richer mine of ideas quickly.

To cluster, take a word or phrase that is central. For instance, you might want to concentrate on childhood memories first. Write "childhood," draw a rough circle around it, and then a line with an arrow off that circle. Then you write the next word that comes to you, whatever it is, and circle that. Continue to arrow off of this word or idea, or go back to the original word ("childhood"), as many times as ideas come to you. When you are done, "childhood" will probably look something like the example below. Whenever you run out of room, take a fresh piece of paper and continue clustering.

3. Another good method that works especially well for visual people is called storyboarding, a process widely used in businesses and organizations. John Trent's book, *LifeMapping*, gives details on how to adapt this technique to a variety of situations.[1] You'll need some tools before you begin: a few packets of notecards in different sizes and different colors (5x7s are one color, 4x6s another, and two different colors for the 3x5 cards), a large surface on which you can pin the notecards (cork, art board, canvas stretched over boards, etc.), and lots of push pins. You'll also need some markers. (Again, visual people often like to use different colors. Have fun with this!)

SAMPLE OF CLUSTERING TECHNIQUE

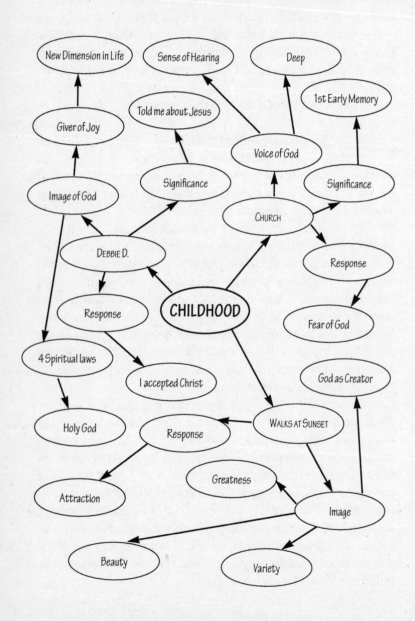

To storyboard your spiritual autobiography, start with your larger cards. For each *experience*, you will use a large (5x7) card. Write down a short phrase that describes the experience. Pin that up on your board. Under that, use a 4x6 card (or more) to describe the *significance* of that event for you, spiritually. Under that, use a 3x5 card in one color for the *image of God* that you formed from that experience, and another color for your *response*. As you go through this, you will have a big, colorful picture of the significant spiritual points in your journey with God to this point. (The actual process of going through the spiritual autobiography will be described below.)

4. Draw scenes or symbols or pictures, alone or in combination with words, to describe your experiences, image of God, and responses. If you choose this technique, either plan on one piece of paper per experience, or a large surface of some sort so you can get an overview. (Or you can later pin up your individual pictures, collage-like, which in itself may become part of the whole experience.)

5. Some people like to talk things out, rather than write or draw. You can take this approach alone, by recording into a tape recorder, or do it with another person. You will want to devote several sessions to the whole process. If you do talk to someone else, I suggest you also tape the sessions, so you can go back to them if needed. It would also be best if that person is either a "spiritual director" or mentor, or someone who is also going through this process.

6. Write it out—journal style, or in letters to God, or in story form. This can also be used in conjunction with 1 and 2 above; you use the former approaches to get the ideas down quickly, then elaborate on each one.

Besides deciding on a technique, you might want to think through your approach to gleaning your ideas. Some will find it easiest to begin chronologically. Others might prefer a more random approach, starting with whatever comes to mind first. You may start at any point in the process as well—by thinking of experiences, or images of God, or relationships or Scriptures or circumstances. The best way is to do it *your way*.

STEP ONE: DEFINE YOUR EXPERIENCE

Now let's begin. Whatever technique you've chosen, you will need to explore experiences that have had a spiritual impact on you. The approach is wholly subjective—that is, look for things that are actually important to you, not things that seem like they should be important. Again, start this by praying that God would bring things to mind that he wants to show you.

At this point you may be wondering how you would know if an experience really was God breaking through. My answer is: Is the experience, or what you learned of God, consistent with what the Bible says God is like? If so, then you can be confident that it was the Holy Spirit bringing Jesus alive to you, as the Bible says he will. If the image of God you gleaned through the experience contradicts Scripture, then that experience does not come from the Holy Spirit.

How do you know if it was God, or just a psychological experience? I'm not really sure it makes a difference. God can work through any means to reveal himself. The key issue to keep coming back to: Did the experience reveal something personally to you about the God that is described in the Bible?

Sometimes the most significant experiences are based on seemingly insignificant things. Jack's experience of turning on the radio those two times and hearing those particular pieces may not have meant much to someone else. But to him, they were very significant.

Ernest Boyer, Jr., in his book *Finding God at Home*, tells how as a young boy he would tug on his great-grandfather's jacket to get his attention when the man was talking to someone. His great-grandfather would finish his sentence, stoop down to Ernest's level, look at him and wait patiently. "As he waited he looked at me with eyes that told me that I need not hurry, that there was time; eyes that said that I need not fear what he would think of what I might say, anything would be fine; eyes that seemed to see the person I most truly was and accept that person. His was caring of the deepest sort." This was a deeply spiritual experience for him, because years later he recalled "what it was like to have been in the full acceptance of those eyes."[2] Quite possibly the adult Ernest Boyer's view of God himself is connected to that experience of being so fully accepted and loved by his great-grandfather.

For your first experience, I encourage you to think back on your very early impressions of God. What were they? Through what did they come?

My first impressions of God include two experiences. One is sitting in church as a small child. What I heard was a booming voice. Since it was a large church, and I was too small to see up front, I thought the voice coming through the loudspeakers was the voice of God himself. I listened. The voice contained authority; the sternness of the tone conveyed to me that here was someone not to be trifled with.

Also under "first impressions" would have to be God as Creator. From when I was very small, I loved the outdoors. There I saw a creative God, someone who had great imagination, great power, and great wisdom and ability to run things. These impressions have lasted; they are the foundations on which my image of God has been built.

Besides your first impressions, you will have other experiences to record. I suggest you also look for:

1. Experiences from *nature*. For instance, one important experience when I felt God touched my life occurred when I was a teenager. I was walking alone on an ocean beach at night, an especially clear night with no moon and bright stars. As I looked up at the sky and out toward the huge waves, I felt two things: God's immensity, and my own insignificance. But then something happened. Though I had been careful to keep a good distance from where the waves lapped the shore—the summer night was a bit chill—suddenly a large wave broke on the shore and the water came all the way up to where I was, gently touching my feet. It felt

almost like a kiss from God. He seemed to be saying, "Yes, I am immense. But you are not insignificant. I have chosen to include you in my immensity. You are a part of my great design." This incident deeply affected how I view God and myself to this day.

2. Experiences involving *significant relationships*. There may be a few people whom God used to help you grow, or comfort you, or challenge you. Perhaps included in this would be an author, speaker or musician whose words or music seemed to touch you just when and where you needed it. I have several people, alive and dead, who have deepened my awareness of God and my own calling.

3. Incidents that were *turning points*—either toward or away from God. These may be major crises, such as the death of a loved one, or more minor events or private events, such as a personal crisis of belief.

4. *Prayer/devotional times*. Perhaps it was a Bible study you did, or a sermon or message you heard, or some special music that held some significance.

You may think of other things. What is important is a sense of *God* in each experience/event/relationship.

STEP TWO: EXPLORE ITS SIGNIFICANCE

The next step is to explore the significance of your experience. Why did this experience mean something to you? In my experience at the ocean, the wave touching my feet seemed to be a reminder that God's great plan included me. The meaning of the experience—what God seemed to be saying to you—is what you want to record.

Sometimes there is more than one reason an experience is significant. For instance, the high-school friend that first witnessed to me was significant for two reasons: She told me about Jesus Christ and introduced me to God's plan of salvation; and she demonstrated the joy of the Lord, such that I was attracted to God. I believe God used her in my life to bring me to him.

STEP THREE: EXPLORE YOUR IMAGE OF GOD

Part of the reason each experience is significant is usually that it shows us something about who God is. Remember, when God breaks through to us it's usually to teach us something about himself and his ways. Even if he shows us something about ourselves in the experience, there is almost always a connection to some aspect of God's character.

For each experience, summarize in a phrase (or picture) at least one image or aspect or characteristic of God connected to that experience. For instance, under my experience of God at the ocean, I put down "God as Creator of great and small" and "love." Under my relationship with Debbie, my high-school friend, I put "Savior," because it was through Debbie that I learned Jesus was my Savior. Also in this area you might want to list any significant Scriptures connected to the experience.

STEP FOUR: DESCRIBE YOUR RESPONSE

In this process we are trying to get a picture of your relationship with God, and relationships are two-way. Therefore it's important to include your response to God in each experience. My response to the "voice of God" as a child in church was a mixture of fear and respect. My response to my beach experience was tears of humility and gratitude. My response to Debbie's witness was to accept Jesus Christ into my life.

Sometimes the response and/or experience may be negative. For instance, one of my experiences involved a betrayal by someone I thought was a friend. When I noticed our relationship was rather one-sided and talked to her about it, she admitted that she had been using me as a guinea pig for her counseling courses, and that she didn't really care as much as she had seemed to. The spiritual significance of this experience for me was it taught me that God doesn't always shelter us from our own naiveté. My response was to be wary of friendships at first. But over time, that wariness was molded into discernment. I learned, ultimately, that God could use even painful experiences for our own maturity.

To summarize, here is what you are looking for as you construct your spiritual autobiography:

- What experiences, events or relationships were spiritually significant in some way?
- Why was each event significant? What did it mean to you? What did you learn from it?
- What key attributes or image of God did you glean from the experience? If there were any relevant Scriptures or hymns, what were they?
- What was your response, positive and/or negative?

LOOKING FOR PATTERNS

Constructing your spiritual autobiography could well become a lifelong process. But after you've recorded at least seven to ten experiences, you can begin to look for patterns. These patterns will make up the unique "love language" that God has used with you in the past. They will give you a vivid portrait of your relationship to God to date.

Remember, when God breaks into our lives it's to show us one or more of the following: who he is, who we are, how he feels about us, what his purpose is, or how we can serve him. Look at your autobiography for the following:

1. One of the Holy Spirit's goals is to point out sin in our lives (John 16:8). Taking your experiences as a whole, are there any weaknesses in your own character that emerge? For instance, my list would include lack of self-acceptance, lack of trust, lack of generosity. Several of the experiences involved God speaking to these character flaws and helping me grow.

One way to look at the character qualities God might be working on is to go through the lists in Galatians 5:19–23. First Paul lists negatives: "sexual immorality, impurity and debauchery; idolatry and witchcraft; hatred, discord, jealousy, fits of rage, selfish ambition, dissensions, factions and envy; drunkenness, orgies and the like." If any of these things are present in our lives, we can be sure the Holy Spirit will be trying to get rid of them.

The positive list of the fruit of the Holy Spirit—love, joy, peace, patience, kindness, goodness, faithfulness, gentleness and self-control—are the qualities God wants to form in us. Perhaps you can link some of your experiences to God changing you, for instance, from an impatient to a more patient person.

2. God often meets us at our point of need, or at a point where he wants to mature us. Ask yourself, What recurring images or characteristics of God are repeated? Has there been any progression as you've matured in your faith? (My images moved from God as Creator to accepting Savior to Guide, persistent lover, healer and more. Recurring images were God as Creator, Healer, Protector, Savior and Lord, Redeemer of pain, Guide, Provider.)

3. What growth points can you see, as recorded in the *my response* sections? Praise God for his work in you, and be encouraged.

4. Do you see any repetition in the *means* God used to communicate with you? What was the primary impression: something seen (an image); words or a sense of voice (audio-linguistic); a feeling or action (kinesthetic); music; a sudden insight or concept; a sense of pattern or understanding? Are these consistent with what you know about your own learning style (see chapter 2)?

We have mentioned that God most often communicates through the Bible, through other Christians, through prayer, and through nature. He also uses circumstances, which we will explore further in the next chapter. Most likely all these means will be represented in your autobiography. But are there one or two means God seemed to use most often? For me, other Christians, prayer (in which I focus on "listening" to God through Scriptures or images he brings to mind), and seeing patterns in nature or circumstances seem to be the main vehicles in which God reaches out to me.

For other people the patterns may be quite different. An informal survey I conducted with more than thirty Christians I know, reveals the range of how God communicates is great. Some examples: nature; seeing significant spiritual changes in one's own life or in others; a spiritual mentor or prayer partner; dreams; corporate worship; Scripture; other people; hymns or other spiritual songs; prayer and meditation; circumstances (God's hand guiding daily experiences); blessings of life; media; seeing God's hand in the larger events in the world; prayer dialogue (one person termed it "an awareness of a voice inside my head, accompanied by assurance that it is *God's* voice"); silence; journaling or other forms of writing; certain authors; the experiences or actions of others (one person mentioned "those who suffer and those who care for them," another "the lives of hymn writers").

What a varied list! God created individual differences, delights in them, and uses them to weave a unique and unrepeatable relationship with each of his people. God initiates; we respond. Taking time to look at God's work in the past is a first step in responding to him and learning his ways. In the next chapter, we'll explore some of the ways we can interpret our circumstances and see God at work around and through us. Armed with this, we'll focus on how to develop a keener awareness of how God might be trying to communicate through the individual aspects of our lives—including our weaknesses and needs.

Chapter Six

FINDING GOD
IN YOUR CIRCUMSTANCES

One day I discovered a medical bill for $279 I hadn't known I owed. Something moved me to look into another file. There I found two uncashed checks totaling almost the amount I needed for the unexpected bill. (It's very unusual for me to leave *any* uncashed checks anywhere, let alone buried in a file, believe me!)

How should I view this somewhat mundane circumstance? Was it God's provision, or just "luck" or "serendipity" or "coincidence"?

Can we expect to find God in the ordinary, mundane aspects of our lives? If we find a parking space just outside the shop we intend to patronize on a day when it's pouring rain, is that God's provision? If we don't, is that God withholding something? Should we pray about such mundane things?

On a more profound level, where is God when things go wrong? When we face illness, or unemployment, or tragedy, is God's hand in those circumstances? What about when we seek him with all we're worth, and he seems utterly silent?

In short, how are we to view God in our circumstances? Do we find him only at unexpected moments, such as the times we explored in our spiritual autobiographies? Or can we expect to encounter him daily, as we go about the mundane activities of commuting and working and making meals and cleaning up and helping our children with homework and attending meetings and fixing broken things? What can we do during difficulties, how do we respond when he seems silent?

I believe we can and should expect to find God daily, in the midst of circumstances both great and small, pleasant and unpleasant. If he is sovereign, he is in control of everything. Our task is to gain his perspective and obey, and in obeying to experience more of God. We are daily writing our own personal histories of God at work as we live our lives. As Dr. Tony Evans says, "God is not revealed in Scripture in formulas, 1A, 1B, 1C. God is revealed in the realities of life. . . . God always reveals himself in historical context, because he's trying to make himself make sense in the arena of men."[1]

To understand how he works in our personal histories, we can look at how he has worked through human history, starting of course with the biblical record.

GOD AT WORK IN HUMAN HISTORY

The biblical record shows that there were times when God broke through human history with spectacular displays of power. Elijah's contest on Mount Carmel, where he challenged the prophets of Baal and God unleashed his power for all to see, is one example (see 1 Kings 18). The book of Acts in the New Testament contains many illustrations of God at work through Christ's disciples: cripples are healed, the dead brought back to life, miraculous escapes from prison are arranged. Throughout church history and to the present day there are records of miraculous physical healings, outpourings of the Holy Spirit leading to revivals, and other signs that God is still at work through the extraordinary. No doubt some of the examples from your own spiritual autobiography are personal examples of God breaking through in some extraordinary way.

Other times God works slowly and mysteriously. "'My thoughts are not your thoughts, neither are your ways my ways,' declares the Lord" in Isaiah 55:8. God sometimes graciously shows us the purpose behind our hardships, as when Joseph saw the big picture and was able to perceive God's sovereign hand in all his difficulties (Genesis 45). But at other times he never explains himself. Why was Peter miraculously delivered from prison by an angel, while John the brother of James was murdered by Herod (Acts 12)? Why was John the Baptist, whom Jesus called the greatest person ever to live, allowed to languish in a prison and then be beheaded so that a king could save face? Hebrews 11 says that some who lived by faith experienced great triumphs, but many others did not. Instead they were tortured, imprisoned, killed. God doesn't always rescue us from difficulties in this life, even if we have great faith.

But when God says in Isaiah 55 that his ways and thoughts are not ours, what does he go on to say? That his word shall accomplish his purposes, that we will experience joy and peace as we participate in his purposes (verses 10–13). He assures us he will work in and through us, according to his word, and that we will experience peace and joy as we participate with him.

Stephen seemed to experience that even as he was being stoned to death (Acts 7:54–60). Numerous accounts of Christian martyrs attest to the fact that even during great suffering, God's presence can be perceived. Perhaps there are examples from your life or someone you know where this experience of God's presence in the face of suffering made him seem all the more real.

But what about when God seems absent, absolutely silent? The biblical record also includes this experience. From the psalmists' cries to the prophets' pleading, it's clear that often, from a human perspective, God seemed absent. So he does in our lives also, at times. Our prayers seem to hit the ceiling and fall back upon us with a thud. We grope our way through a dark tunnel, with no obvious light at the other end. This is undoubtedly how

Job felt, as he tried to make sense of all the disasters that befell him and, worst of all, God's seeming silence.

But even then, even with Job or the psalmists or the prophets, the larger record shows that though God seemed absent, he was still at work. Job didn't know it, but we are shown in the first chapter that Job's trials were part of a much larger cosmic contest. And God restored Job's fortunes in the end. We are shown the reasons Jeremiah went through so much agony—he, along with his people, was experiencing God's judgment on sin by being sent into exile.

It takes faith to believe that God is at work when he seems so silent. But we can rest in the assurance from the scriptural record that when such times come, there is always a reason, even if we can't see it.

That is what everything seems to come down to: faith. It takes faith even to see God at work through the mundane. One demonstration is in how God provided food for the prophet Elijah through the faith of a widow. At Elijah's word, this widow used the last of her flour and oil to make bread for him—and found that the flour and oil didn't run out for three years. Jesus took a boy's meager lunch and fed a crowd of five thousand. It seems that everyday acts, transformed by faith, can become extraordinary means of God's grace.

Jesus also taught much about the kingdom of God using examples from ordinary life. "He who puts into practice my words is like the wise man who built his house on the rock. . . ." (Matthew 7:24). The kingdom of God is like a woman who lost a coin . . . like a man who sowed seed in his field . . . like a mustard seed . . . like yeast . . . like a landowner who hired men to work in his field . . . like a king preparing a wedding banquet for his son. We can find God and learn of his ways as we pay attention to the ordinary experiences of our lives, using the eyes of faith.

I'll give you an example from my own life. One night my small son woke up, calling for me. He said he'd had a scary dream. I thought back to that evening: Gene and I had quarreled.

David had heard and called down from his bedroom, "Quit fighting!" We don't argue that often, and when we do it upsets David. I realized that David's bad dream probably had some connection to the quarrel.

So I tried to speak to David's real fears, that he is too immature to understand. I told him about how we are a family, we are here to love and help each other. Sometimes we argue, sometimes we get mad at each other, but we still love each other.

I stayed with him, singing and stroking his hair, his back, soothing him to sleep. Though I was exhausted myself, it became a sweet time. The week had been hectic, filled with lots of activities and things to attend to. I had not spent much time alone with God. That night, I felt as if God were nurturing and soothing me, even as I nurtured and soothed David. The simple songs and hymns I sang bolstered *my* faith. It was as if God were loving both David and me through me. I learned that I can meet God, not only during the times of solitude, but through the times of loving my family as well.

David wanted me to stay with him. I couldn't, for his good and mine. I sang, rubbed his back for a while. Then I quit touching him, only sang. Then I got up and slowly left the room, singing as I went. I was weaning him of my immediate presence, while assuring him I was still near if he needed me.

As I drifted back to sleep, I pondered the experience. David thought he was afraid of monsters, but I suspected he was really feeling insecure because of the argument. How often when I think my problem is one thing, is it really another? I pray for a bigger house that would better meet my needs, and God shows me verses on his presence. I pray for my husband to become more of a leader in our home and God convicts me of my own problem with control. (Who am I to say where Gene needs to grow? That's God's business.) Perhaps I am just like a little child, too immature to know my real needs or fears. God in his wisdom speaks to the real issues on the deepest levels, even as I tried to reassure David about what I suspected was his real fear.

And is it possible that God sometimes has to wean us of a sense of his immediate presence, though he is still near? Just as I slowly withdrew from David so he could sleep—though I myself remained only a few feet away—perhaps God sometimes seems to withdraw for our own good, even though he is very near.

Since I began looking for God's grace notes in my everyday life, hardly a day has gone by when I don't experience some example of it. But more about that in the next chapter. For now, let's look at some of the ways God may use circumstances in our lives for his purposes. Then we'll focus on how we may respond to God in a variety of different circumstances.

HOW GOD MAY USE CIRCUMSTANCES

God works through our circumstances because he is always active in our lives and in our world. Understanding how he uses circumstances can help us discern his hand.

The first way God uses circumstances is to get our attention. When something unusual happens, for better or worse, our attention often turns to God. Sometimes "coincidences" seem nothing short of miraculous. In such situations, we can either praise and thank God, or shrug it off as happenstance. If it is something good, and in tune with what we know of God from the Bible, I believe we should thank God for it. I think we should pray for discernment in any unusual circumstance. It just may be God's way of getting our attention.

Sometimes the only way God can get our attention, unfortunately, is through pain. I can't help but wonder if that's because when life just hums along, too often we tune God out. I notice, for instance, that Christians often don't bring up prayer requests for things that they think they should be able to handle themselves. They only pray for the things that are obviously beyond them. If God desires a relationship with us most of all, and relationships are nurtured by communication, can we blame him if he sometimes resorts to allowing difficult circumstances into our lives? If that's the only way we will turn to him, perhaps that is why he allows them.

Walt, a scientist working in research and development for a large oil corporation, now looks back on how God used difficulties to get his attention. For nineteen years, Walt held the perfect job. He had complete freedom to do what he loved to do. But changes in the corporation—a new boss who constantly criticized, downsizing, backbiting among employees—slowly turned what had been a warm, fuzzy security blanket into a hard straitjacket. Walt became obsessed with his job. His emotions were blunted—he couldn't feel, couldn't laugh, couldn't cry. He found it hard to pay attention even in church. He was irritable with everyone. "Finally I prayed that God would release me from these circumstances," Walt says. But somehow, he wasn't ready for God's answer to his prayer: being terminated. He had always been told he was such a valued employee, he never dreamed they would let him go.

Suddenly Walt was plunged into a whole new world, a world of uncertainty, a world of dependency on God, a world of needing to reach out to people. The lessons he learned over seven months of job searching, he says he wouldn't trade for anything, though they were extremely hard. God got Walt's attention through a difficult situation.

Sometimes God uses circumstances to convict us of sin. When I went through a particularly painful time during my husband's unemployment, God used it to show me how self-sufficient I had tried to become. My self-sufficiency was sinful because it kept me from depending on God as I should, and it kept me from interacting with other believers as I should. God used that difficult time to help me see my own sin.

We have to be careful not to interpret other people's difficulties as God's way of getting their attention. But when we are faced with circumstances that throw us off balance, it's always appropriate to pray for God to show us what we're to learn. Because that's the second way God uses circumstances: to teach us.

God often shows us something about himself or ourselves through circumstances. Walt learned that it was a mistake to depend on any human organization for his security. He was humbled by the goodness of others, by their eagerness to reach out and support him. And he experienced firsthand the biblical truth that "God is light; in him there is no darkness at all" (1 John 1:5).

That is another way God uses circumstances: to mature us, to help us grow up in faith. Sometimes the only way that can happen is to teach us to walk by faith, not by sight, through difficulties. As Walt said, "Because God is light, he can see the way when I can't." How else could Walt discover that experientially, except by learning to trust God through his dark time?

God doesn't only teach us or mature us through the hard times, however. God also uses circumstances simply to bless us, to bring good into our lives. I can't tell you how many times, in the writing of this book, that God used something I heard or saw or read to encourage me.

I know many people say that they only really get to know God, or know him best, through the hard times. I have known his care through some hard times, so I understand what they're saying. But for me, God's blessings have had at least as powerful an impact in melting me and helping me to trust God. Perhaps because I experienced so little of simple goodness and grace in my background, when I experience that from God it does something deep within me. It is during those circumstances of complete grace that I sense best that he loves me, and my trust in his love nature grows.

One incident that stands out in my mind is the Friday evening my friend Charlene called and said, "I just got this impulse to invite you and Gene out to dinner tonight. I'd really like to do that. If you can get a baby-sitter, let's go. You pick the place."

It was 5:20 and, unusual for me, I hadn't started making supper. My baby-sitter could come over. We went out and had a marvelous time.

What was especially wonderful, though, was the timing of the incident. The following Wednesday, a couple who had been my spiritual parents during college were planning to come through town. I hadn't seen them in many years, and they'd never met Gene or David. John and Betty said they'd like to take us out to dinner. Now, I can't even remember any other time when someone has taken us out to dinner. When Charlene called on Friday night to make her offer, I thought, "I can't believe it! Being taken out to dinner two times within one week!"

But as it turned out, John and Betty never did take us out to dinner. The night before that planned event, I entered the hospital for preterm labor. I spent nine days there, trying to keep my baby from being born prematurely. I couldn't help but think that Charlene's impulse to take us out to dinner that Friday night came directly from God, as she was sensitive to his Spirit. God gave us a wonderful gift through her generosity. He knew how special it was to me for a friend to invite us out to dinner. And Charlene has been one of God's special people in my life. The whole incident also encouraged me that indeed, my times (and my baby's) were in God's hands—even if things turned out differently than I'd planned.

A final way God may use circumstances is to guide us. Here we need to be especially prayerful so we can discern what he is trying to tell us. I don't think it's wise to trust circumstances alone for figuring out what God wants us to do. It's best to approach circumstances with much prayer. When circumstances line up with God's other means of guidance—the Bible, an inner sense of peace and conviction from the Holy Spirit, and the affirmation from God's people—then you can trust that you've got the right message.

RESPONDING TO GOD IN OUR CIRCUMSTANCES

In order to experience God in our circumstances, we need to know how to respond. When we respond rightly, we deepen our relationship with him. We enlarge our capacity to experience his nature and participation in our lives.

The first thing to know is that we are never to let our circumstances color our view of God. Our knowledge of God is to inform how we view our circumstances, not the other way around. If we view God from the middle of our circumstances, we will always get a distorted, or at least incomplete, picture of God.

Recall the image in Exodus of God leading his people in the form of a cloud by day, a pillar of fire by night. In order for the people to see him clearly, he needed to reveal himself in contrast to their circumstances: by day it was easiest to see a cloud; against the dark of the night they needed light (the pillar of fire).

Note that the cloud hid everything it covered. You couldn't see beyond it, or through it—the cloud obscured everything else. The people were just to follow the cloud. When God leads, he often obscures the way, but wants us to follow *him* in faith.

So no matter what the circumstance—good, bad, or mundane—the main thing is to seek God himself. God's goal is to have you grow in your relationship with him. He's not interested in your learning a set of rules. He wants you to know him and trust him most of all.

RESPONSE TO DIFFICULTIES

Life is difficult. Jesus warned us it would be so. Trouble comes in any number of guises: ill health, financial problems, rebellious children, abusive parents, broken relationships, the daily grind of single parenthood, tragedies of every stripe: fatal car accidents, floods and fires, accidental drownings, drive-by shootings, etc. And God does not shelter the believer from these effects of a bent world. Yet, when such trials come, we have a choice: either to turn toward him and experience deeper truths of God, or turn away and ask, "Why me?"

Sanna Baker could easily have asked that question. She had battled cancer for seven and a half years, cancer that ravaged breast, brain, liver and bone. Yet she clung tenaciously to life. In a talk she gave to women in her church, Sanna shared her response to her suffering. "I am thankful that I do not carry the burden of wondering, 'Why me?'" Sanna said. She explained how in her growing up years she would watch the Minnesota skies, drink in the beauty of "color boiling up into the skies after the sun had dropped below the horizon," marvel at the curtains of Northern Lights and the countless stars that swelled the dark skies at night. "It bred into my bones a sense of the greatness of the Creator," Sanna said. "If this God, who created all of this, is my God, all there is for me to do is what Job ultimately did: He bowed himself before the Lord, saying, 'I know that thou canst do all things, and that no purpose is beyond thee.'

"I can live not knowing all the answers, not understanding all of the whys, because I know that the One who calls the stars by name knows my name, and I am precious to him. Who could I better trust with my life? The whys melt away."

Sanna recalled some key Scriptures: "Jesus told us to expect tribulation in this world (John 16:33). But he also says, 'Be of good cheer. I have overcome the world. I am the resurrection and the life. Because I live, ye shall live also. I will be with you even unto the end of the world.' I will be with you."

Sanna clung to these words. She had learned that, like an anchor in the storm that keeps a boat from dashing against the rocky shore, the promises of God hold up during the storms of life. Sanna could lean on God and not her own understanding during her suffering because she was looking at God not through the lens of her current circumstances, but through her understanding of who the Bible and her own past experiences say he is.

Especially when we are in difficult times, it helps to look back on the examples from the Bible and our own lives where God has proven himself faithful. We can cling to these, test them as anchors in the storm. As Dan Allender and Tremper Longman point out in their book, *Cry of the Soul*, "Memory plays a crucial role in the Bible. It has an important role to play in faith. . . . Memory is a creative borrowing of the past as a template of what we hope for the present. To remember the past is to reshape the present with desire and hope."[2]

Looking back on God's faithfulness as mirrored in the Bible stories, and calling on God to save us likewise, has biblical precedence (see Psalms 74:2 and 77:11). Remembering times he has been faithful in our own pasts, as we did in constructing a spiritual autobiography, is also biblical. When Samuel was judge over Israel, the Philistines attacked. But God helped the Israelites to defeat their enemies. Samuel set up a stone in a certain place, calling it "Ebenezer"—stone of help—as a reminder that God had helped them to that point.

That is what we have done with our spiritual autobiographies: set up our own personal "Ebenezers." It's not that we lean on the experiences themselves, hoping that God will work in the same way. Rather, we put our weight on the characteristics of God that are illuminated by the Scripture or the experience.

So the first thing to do in difficult times is to look to God as the Scriptures and our own histories reveal him.

KEEP TALKING TO GOD

The second thing is to keep communicating with God. Remember, he is after a relationship with us. In any relationship, there are misunderstandings that have to be cleared up. Feelings need to be aired and worked through. You don't understand what is happening? Talk to God about it, even as Moses, Job and the psalmists did. These men of God didn't hide their pain, confusion, even anger at God about their circumstances. They brought them to God. When Moses was fed up with the Israelites' complaints, he cried out to God (Exodus 17:4). Job, overcome with the loss of everything he had—family, wealth, health—poured out his feelings and complaints to God. The Psalms are full of expressions of such emotions as pain (Psalm 6), grief, loneliness, fear (Psalm 22, 35, 55), even bargaining (Psalms 88, 77)—to name just a few.

You're angry, fearful, lonely, confused? Tell God all about it! Keep communicating, even when he seems silent. Perhaps he is silent to allow you to work through your feelings, as a good counselor might. (One of his names, after all, is Wonderful Counselor [Isaiah 9:6].)

Be honest before God, but seek his perspective as well. Pray for the Holy Spirit to help you understand what you are to learn from this. Pore over the Scriptures for perspective and promises to claim. Talk to sensitive, godly people through whom God can work to bring his comfort and perspective.

Then, do whatever it is that you know to do, that you sense God is telling you. Eventually, the cloud will break. You may never understand completely what God is doing or why, but you will in one way or another find God. That is the biblical witness, and the testimony of countless other Christians.

When my husband went through some rocky times of unemployment and underemployment, I didn't understand what was happening or why. I didn't know what to do to help him. The strain on us as individuals and on our marriage tested our commitment to each other and to God. We felt alone.

I cried out to God many times during that dark period, which lasted more than a few months. I clung to Scriptures like Jeremiah 29:11–14 as my own personal promise, and I looked back on times when God had been my helper and deliverer. This faith sustained me.

I tried to be faithful to God, but I wasn't always honest with myself or him about my feelings. Slowly, however, I realized that I needed to be completely honest with God about how I felt. The more I opened up about my confusion, pain and fear, the more real God seemed to be. He brought people to me who offered hope. Somehow new strength flowed into me.

Eventually I came to glimpse ways God was changing me through this hard time. That gave a sense of meaning to my struggles. I began to reach out to other couples who were going through employment struggles, which eventually led to writing *Men in Search of Work and the Women Who Love Them*. God showed me how he was redeeming our struggles, according to 2 Corinthians 1:4–5, where Paul talks about how God comforts us in all our troubles so that we, in turn, can comfort others with the same comfort we have received from God.

And God became real to me in a new way.

Trouble brings us to a crisis of faith, where we have to decide whether we will believe our circumstances or what the Scriptures teach us about God. Depending on what we believe, we will either turn away from or toward God. If we turn toward him, we will, somehow in some way, come to experience more of him.

But sometimes on the way, we have to cross a dry, barren spiritual desert. What do we do when no matter how hard we seek him, he seems to be totally absent?

RESPONDING TO GOD IN THE DRY TIMES

Most Christians experience, at one time or another, periods when we can see nothing of God's hand, when his goodness seems to have abandoned us. Our prayers feel like they bounce off the ceiling. The Bible seems a dry and dusty tome that has nothing to do with us now. Perhaps our emptiness stems from a tragedy that we just can't believe God could let happen if he truly loved us. Perhaps it's just the dailyness of life that has ground us down. Sometimes there is no obvious reason for God's apparent distance.

I have experienced such times. And I have to be honest, I never did receive any great insight or new sense of God. My desert experiences have simply taught me to persevere, despite lack of feelings or revelations about God. And I believe that may well have been the point, the reason God allowed those times. Periodically, I have to be reminded that "we live by faith, not by sight" (2 Corinthians 5:7). It's possible to become too dependent on the signposts along the way that speak of God's presence. It is good of him to provide such signposts, it is right for us to note and recall them, but we have to remember God is not the signpost.

Elijah seemed to need this reminder. After his great contest on Mount Carmel, where God decisively showed that he, not Baal, was the Lord, Elijah ran for his life from Jezebel, who vowed to kill him. Depleted, he sank down under a broom tree and asked God to take his life. God sent an angel to feed him and give him water. Sleep, food and water revived Elijah, and he ran away to a cave at Horeb, the mountain of God. God came to him that night. A great and powerful wind passed by, but Scripture says that God was not in the wind. Then there was an earthquake, but God was not in the earthquake. After the earthquake, a fire came, but God was not in the fire. Then a gentle whisper beckoned. It was God.

Elijah became used to seeing God in the spectacular—wind, earthquake, fire. He apparently also needed to know that God was in the "small, still voice" or the whisper that comes gently.

Often, I think I need to be reminded that God is God. He is not like me. Too often my agenda is not on the same page as his. He has big, big purposes, beyond me. Lest I get too attached to the joys he can and does bring, he sometimes withdraws those. At such times, I wonder if he's asking, "Can you be content with me, me alone, apart from my good gifts?"

If I use the dark or dry times to persevere in seeking God, and God alone, I am always eventually rewarded. "Suffering produces perseverance; perseverance, character; and character, hope. And hope does not disappoint us, because God has poured out his love into our hearts by the Holy Spirit, whom he has given us" (Romans 5:3–5).

But trouble isn't the only time to look for God. The good times bring their own set of challenges and opportunities to find God.

RESPONDING IN THE GOOD TIMES

Part of the reason so many of us ask, "Why me?" when we encounter stormy seas is because we have a distorted view of reality. Unconsciously we assume that life is supposed to be easy. We don't like to hear that life is difficult, that we should expect hardships as a matter of course. We spend lots of time and energy trying to deny that this is the case.

A more biblical perspective is that the whole world is off-balance, bent, fallen—because of sin, because humankind has chosen to go its own way. Since everything is off kilter, lots of times innocent people suffer from tragedies like natural disasters, disease, and famine. Innocent people also suffer directly from the sins of others, as when a terrorist blows up a building or a child is victimized by an adult.

Why do I bring all this up under the heading of "responding to God's goodness"? Because if we expect the world to be full of trouble, even evil, when we see goodness and grace we will realize its true source: God. "Don't be deceived, my dear brothers. Every good and perfect gift is from above, coming down from the Father of the heavenly lights, who does not change like shifting shadows," says James 1:16–17. Don't be deceived into thinking that things are supposed to go right, and raise your fist at God when things go wrong. Realize that sin is at work everywhere in the world, and stop in wonderment whenever you see any modicum of good. Stop and realize that it is God at work in his world.

When you see someone committing a random act of kindness, rejoice. Even if that person is an unbeliever, that act is sparked by the image of God that is stamped on the soul of every human being.

When the rain comes down in the right amounts—not too much, not too little, so that fields of corn and wheat flourish and cattle graze—rejoice, for the God of creation is graciously pouring out his blessing on the good and the bad. The world may deserve droughts and floods, but God doesn't let those prevail always.

When God brings wealth or good health or recognition or love into your life, thank him. Praise him for his grace and generosity. Record the times of blessings in your autobiography. Tell others of the wonderful works of the Lord. Hold the gifts lightly, sharing them with others, while you hold tightly to the Giver's hand.

And realize that this time of blessing may be your season of greatest spiritual vulnerability.

THE HIDDEN PERIL OF GOOD TIMES

It was Job's blessings that attracted Satan to challenge Job's sincerity before God. "Take all the good things away from him, and he will curse you to your face," Satan told God. God allowed Satan to test Job.

"How hard it is for a rich man to enter the kingdom of God!" Jesus exclaimed, adding, "It is easier for a camel to go through the eye of a needle than for a rich man to enter the kingdom of God" (Mark 10:23, 25). It is when we are "rich," when we have experienced God's goodness, that we can be most prone to turning away from God. Before Moses died, God told him that when the people entered the promised land and began to thrive, they would reject the Lord (Deuteronomy 31:20). Then God would have to judge them by bringing disasters and difficulties.

When things go well, take extra care to give God the credit and to draw near to him. Realize it may all be gone tomorrow. Acknowledge that you're just as dependent on God as when you weren't so blessed. This can be a time of great strengthening of your faith if you let it.

FINDING GOD IN THE MUNDANE

For most of us, times of great blessing or painful difficulties are punctuated by long stretches of ordinary existence. We secure an education, buy a house, get married, find jobs, raise children, do housework, attend church, sit on committees, take vacations. In any given week, most of us work, fix and clean up meals, help with homework, clean the house, repair our cars, houses, appliances, go to meetings. We watch TV, read the newspaper, meet a friend for lunch, go to the park with the kids. Some of us even take time to read the Bible and pray. Can we find God in the midst of all this humdrum?

I believe we can, if we learn to pay attention. Looking for God's "grace notes" scattered through my everyday life has become one of the greatest joys of my own life. It is "living by God's surprises," as author Harold Myra's book title suggests. How to develop this spiritual awareness is the subject of the next chapter.

Part Three

DEVELOPING
SPIRITUAL
AWARENESS

Chapter Seven

SEEKING GOD

"I hate this house," my four-year-old announced one night at bedtime. "Can we move?"

My heart sank. "What do you hate about this house?" I asked.

"It's too small," he answered.

Now where did he get that notion? Was it my own comments in moments of frustration? Was it that already he's making comparisons with the houses of his friends?

I said to him, "There are good things about small houses, you know."

"Like what?" he asked skeptically.

I shot a brief prayer up to God for wisdom. And the words came to me: "Well, you know how you don't like to be alone? With our house, I can always hear you wherever I am. If you need me, I'm there right away. You know now that I'll be right in the next room as you go to sleep." (My office is in the adjacent bedroom, and I go there to work when he goes to bed.) "And you know how you don't like to sleep alone? When the baby comes, you can share a room, and you'll never have to be alone."

David seemed satisfied—at least for the moment. I kissed him goodnight and retired to my office. There I sought God about this matter.

You see, I myself had been frustrated by our small quarters. When Gene and I bought our first house, we were coming from a three-room apartment with two closets in the whole place. This house was perfect for our needs at the time: three bedrooms, kitchen, dining room, living room, family room, two baths. So what if the closets were all very small—didn't we have five of them now? Most of the yard was slope, but the tiny lot boasted three huge oak trees and several bushes. So what if there wasn't a lot of actual yard space—there was less to mow. It had the feel of being in the woods. Growing up in New England, my dream had always been to have a house in the woods.

Eight years later, our circumstances have totally changed. We've added two children, and I work from home. With baby paraphernalia and my active, pack-rat older son's "stuff" (today he tried to get me to promise never to throw away any of "his" Sunday comics) to accommodate—not to mention room for my office and the projects I'm involved in—the space seems inadequate.

Moving would be the obvious solution—but fluctuating interest rates and other factors make that untenable, at least for the moment. Even while I continue to pray about that option, I have been asking God to open my eyes to what he wants to show me in my present circumstance.

His answers have come readily and wonderfully.

GOD'S MESSAGES IN MY PROBLEM

First, God showed me how to find solutions by clarifying the real problem and defining what I wanted. What I want is a clutter-free house and office I can work in. Once I defined the real problem and my objective, other options besides moving came to mind. Like getting more organized, learning creative ways to use space and problem-solve.

Second, he convicted me of sin. I realized how much my griping about space burdened my husband. I vowed not to say another complaining word about it.

Third, he showed me how he was using the problem in my life. In this case, this unwelcome circumstance is forcing me to become more organized, resourceful, frugal and creative in using what I have. These are valuable lessons for me to learn, and no doubt valuable lessons to pass on to my children.

Fourth, God showed me how to be thankful. I first thanked him for what he was teaching me through this situation. Then I began to feel thankful for what I did have. I would not have been able to answer David's question adequately had God not opened up my eyes to what he has provided.

Fifth, I learned something else invaluable: how our view of circumstances can change when we seek God's perspective.

A few weeks later, David said at breakfast, "Tell me again why it's good to live in a small house."

This time I was ready. "We can always hear each other and talk to each other, even if we're in different rooms. And you'll get to share a room with the baby. If we had a big house, I'd have to spend more time cleaning it and there would be less time to do fun things together. And because we have a smaller house, we have more money to do fun things together, or buy neat things at garage sales like the toys we got the other day." (He's still young enough to get away with that one.) "And this particular house is cool because we have woods nearby where we can explore, and lots of birds and wild animals to watch. And we have nice neighbors." All these were things God had opened my own eyes to see.

David thought a moment, then announced, "I used to want to move, but now I think I like this house. I want to stay."

Thank you God, I breathed in my soul. My son's words expressed my own heart.

SEEKING GOD EVERYWHERE

Jeremiah talks about the person who "will not see when something good comes" (God's Word, 17:6). In the previous verse he defines such a person: "the one who trusts in man, who depends on flesh for his strength and whose heart turns away from the Lord." Are we seeking God in everything we experience? Do we really believe he is at work in our lives all the time?

God's gifts and his messages are all around us, like the sound waves our radios and televisions can pick up. The question is, are we tuned in? Is the radio even on? And are we paying attention as we go through our days?

WHAT HINDERS US FROM HEARING GOD

Preset expectations. One of the main reasons we don't hear God's voice in our everyday lives is we don't expect him to speak. We don't think of the whole of our lives as being of concern to God. We compartmentalize what is "spiritual" and what is simply ordinary. During "spiritual times"—when we're reading the Bible, or praying, or in church, we expect God to speak. But we don't expect him to speak through the frustration of locking ourselves out of the house, or through the honest words of our spouse, or the penetrating question of our child, or an everyday act such as putting together a salad.

Yet God does speak through any and all such circumstances. I have either read about or heard of or personally experienced God at work in each of the above situations.

But if we have preset expectations about how he will or won't speak, or what he will or won't say, we obviously won't be tuned in to what he is trying to tell us. He is always with us, even to the end of the age, he promises. We are to walk by the Spirit. If our whole lives are to be lived before him, he will use our whole lives to communicate back to us.

Low self-esteem. Sometimes we may not believe he will speak personally to us, in the midst of our particular circumstances, because we lack the self-esteem to believe he cares about the details of our lives. After all, he has a big universe to run; why should he really bother with my little problems and concerns? When we're feeling this way, we may only seek God during the really tough times, or find ourselves praying for other people's (big) problems.

The antidote to this is to meditate on such Scriptures as Psalm 139, where David catalogs God's knowledge of him: God knows when he sits down and when he gets up, what his thoughts and words will be, where he will go, what he would be—even before David himself knows. Jesus said that even the very hairs of our head are numbered, that not a sparrow falls to the ground without God taking note—and we are worth more than many sparrows (Matthew 10:29–30). Yes, God is infinite and great, and he takes care of great matters. That this great God also cares about, and seeks to use, every detail of our lives is one of the greatest messages of the Bible. "Ears that hear and eyes that see—the Lord has made them both," declares Proverbs 20:12. If you don't hear or see, it's not because God isn't trying to get through.

Our own emotions or problems. Sometimes we can't hear God because we are embroiled in our own emotions or problems. Perhaps we're angry at God, and in our anger we're shutting him out. Or we're so worried about something that it's consuming our lives, and we can't seem to let go of it and let God have his way. Perhaps it's fear that's holding us back—fear of what God will say or how he will lead. Or false guilt over something may keep his real message from getting through.

There was a period when I suffered false guilt because of some wrong teaching. I was involved in a church that believed all women should only be homemakers. My husband struggled at the time with his employment. I was told that I should quit the job I enjoyed, because it was interfering with my husband's ability to "take leadership" and "be the head of the household." I not only felt guilty, I was very confused.

Finally one day I went for a walk and really prayed about it. As I prayed, it seemed that God was telling me these dear people who were advising me were wrong. I countered, "What about all the Scriptures they use in defense?" He answered by showing me other Scriptures that spoke of grace and freedom, and he gave me a different perspective on my husband's struggles. During that prayer session God not only freed me from my false guilt, but he set me on a path of listening for him and learning to discern his voice above that of well-meaning Christians.

Our own deep desires can also lead us astray. When I was a new Christian, I once received a "vision" of my life being joined to my boyfriend's. Astoundingly, independently he had a similar experience. We even received Scriptures that seemed to confirm our future together.

But it was not to be. In college, he turned away from the Lord. I hung on to the relationship for too long because of that "vision." It also confused my walk with the Lord. I doubted my ability to trust any kind of "signs"—and no doubt missed many good things God wanted to show me. Eventually, however, I realized that my own spiritual and emotional immaturity were involved. Had I talked to an older, wiser Christian about it, I probably would have seen more clearly what was going on.

Whenever we're too involved in our own feelings or problems, the place to begin is to bring them before the Lord. Work it through with the Wonderful Counselor. Seek perspective from a wise Christian, if it seems necessary. Don't let anything get in the way of your relationship with God. As you keep the lines of communication open, he will eventually speak.

Past mistaken interpretations. Wrong interpretation of a past experience of God speaking can cause us to doubt whether we can trust our own impressions. Just as my misinterpretation of God's voice made me doubt my inability to hear him, you can be led to shut out his voice if you've had an experience where you thought it was God and you later realized it wasn't.

A dear friend of mine was struggling to keep together a marriage that was being destroyed by her husband's mental illness. One night, after a terrible argument which led her husband to leave the house, she went out onto her porch. She cried her heart out before the Lord, praying that her husband would come back. An unmistakable impression came upon her: "It will be all right."

"But my marriage won't work, there are too many problems!" she cried out to God.

Again, the impression came—like a voice from inside, firmer this time. "It will be all right." My friend was calmed. She knew it was the Lord speaking, and took the message to mean that God would heal her marriage.

But the marriage continued to deteriorate, despite my friend's best efforts. Finally, as divorce seemed the only option, she struggled with guilt and confusion. Was that message really from God? Had he let her down? Could she ever trust that inner voice again? That would be the deepest loss—to go through life not trusting that still voice within her.

Then she realized: The message was not, "I will restore your marriage." That was her interpretation. The words were, "It will be all right." She realized that she had wrongly interpreted God's message because of her own deep desire. God had simply promised that everything would be all right. As she leaned on those words, she began to experience their truth. Everything indeed was all right, even though she got divorced. Again and again she saw him work in her life to provide encouragement, work, money—everything she needed, when she needed it. She began to see that everything was indeed all right because God was with her, and God cared about every need. My friend has incredible stories to tell about God's grace to her, and she does tell them. Thus God is glorified, and he has fulfilled his personal promise to her on that dark night.

If you think you've misinterpreted a message from God, don't shut him out in the future. Go back to him and ask what went wrong. Did you misunderstand what he was really saying, as my friend did? Did you fail to confirm the outer sign with other ways God leads—Scripture, wise counsel of godly people, and an inner conviction? Clarify your misunderstanding with the Lord, just as you would in any other close relationship.

Environmental static. Another reason we may not hear God's voice is that there's too much static in our lives. Simple busyness can cram out time to listen and watch for God. Too many commitments, too much actual noise, too much mental clutter—these things can drown out any messages God may be trying to give us.

Sometimes my agenda is so full of things to do and people to see that I don't really want God to step in, lest he sidetrack me. What if he thinks listening to my neighbor on the phone is more important than meeting my deadline? Not that I consciously think this, but I can tell by my anxiety when something interferes with my plan that I really was not open to God leading me in another direction. When I'm very busy, I'm more apt to hope that God will bless my agenda than to be open to his leading in another direction.

Not all environmental static is controllable. When I had my second child, for the first few months I was so tired and so busy that on some days I barely gave a thought to God, or anything else but surviving. But even then, I discovered that it's always possible to tune in to God. Our inner attitude is the key. One day, after a night of being up every hour with one child or the other, I wondered how I was going to physically and mentally make it through the day. I told God, "I'm going to literally have to take things minute by minute, and I need you to help me survive." I defined surviving as doing what absolutely needed doing (taking care of the baby, not crashing the car, getting dinner together), and not losing my temper at my children or husband. Not only did God help me survive in these ways, he also provided specific encouragement through a newsletter that came in the mail. In that newsletter, two other mothers shared their stories, and it was exactly what I needed to hear at that moment.

Lack of humility. We may believe that "God helps those who help themselves" and so fail to depend on him in our daily pursuits. (By the way, these words are not found anywhere in the Bible.) As we shall see, lack of dependence shuts down our ability to hear God. We tune in to God when we realize that he is the vine, we are the branches, and apart from him we truly can do nothing (John 15:5).

I experience this truth whenever I write. When I feel pretty confident of what I'm going to say—confident enough to forget to seek God—I soon find myself floundering. When I acknowledge to God that I need his help to write anything worthwhile, even if I'm not sure how to start, the words begin to flow.

Disobedience. When we sin, we cut ourselves off from God. We can't expect to hear God if we're having an affair, or harboring resentment, or indulging in gossip. It was only when I confessed to God that I resented my financial situation—including where I lived—that he showed me some of the positive things I mentioned to my son.

Not that we can expect to be free from sin in this life. All of us sin; we can't expect to be perfect. But when we do sin, the Holy Spirit brings it to our attention. If we're listening to him, we will confess the sin and so restore fellowship with God.

It's when God points out our sin and we refuse to listen that we shut ourselves off from his voice in all areas. More subtle than outright disobedience, however, is when he speaks and we don't obey, because we simply don't like what we hear. If we continue to turn a deaf ear to God's messages, that is what we will have— a deaf ear.

Lack of practice. When we're born again, it's as if God gives us rabbit ears to tune into his messages. But it takes practice to learn what his voice sounds like above all others. If we don't practice, for any of the reasons above, then we will be unskilled at listening.

To become a good listener, we have to begin practicing a set of attitudes. As we do, these hindrances will fall away or be overcome by our positive action. Let's look at what these attitudes are.

WHAT IT TAKES TO HEAR GOD

A passion for God. We won't ever get to know God better unless we truly want to know him. And we probably won't want to know him better unless we realize, deep within ourselves, that he is a Person who loves us and wants to walk with us through each hour and minute of each day. If we respond to God as if he were a collection of rules to follow, instead of a Person who loves us and desires to communicate with us, we will unconsciously find ways to avoid him.

Sitting in a group of believers one day, the conversation turned to what we had heard about revival at Christian colleges. Apparently there has been a lot of confession of sin and hurt going on as part of this revival. Someone in the group said, "That just doesn't sound right to me. I would never do that in a group." Someone else said, "That's just the point. You wouldn't do it naturally. But if the Holy Spirit is at work, you would find the courage, if that's what he wanted."

To which the first person replied, "But aren't we good enough already? Don't we have enough of God without all that?"

Someone answered, echoing the words that were in my own heart, "Do we ever have enough of God?"

If we think we have enough of God, something is wrong. He is way too big and wonderful to ever know fully. If our passion to know and love and hear God begins to cool, we need to pray for God to rekindle it. Then we need to spend good time in the Scripture, with whatever method brings it most alive, so that God the Holy Spirit can open our eyes to the wonderful things in the Word.

"Blessed are the pure in heart, for they will see God" (Matthew 5:8). Purity of heart is to want one thing above all else: God. Our relationship with him is that pearl of great price, that is worth more than anything else in our lives. "You will seek me and find me when you seek with all your heart" (Jeremiah 29:13).

Humility and submission. God comes to those who are willing to let him be God, even if they don't understand what he is doing in their lives. He speaks when we are willing to do whatever he says. This is not always easy, because sometimes he tells us things we would rather not hear. Often when I pray about a problem, particularly in a relationship, God points out that I am a big part of the problem. I don't want to see my own failure, but pointing out sin and helping me to grow is part of the Holy Spirit's role.

A friend of mine received a call from her son's teacher, who told her that her son had been misbehaving all week. My friend prayed about the matter. The Lord showed her that her son's behavior was due to the stress level at home. My friend was working two part-time jobs, and her husband was often gone at night for his work. She felt the Lord was telling her to quit one of her jobs. Unfortunately, the job she was to quit was the one she enjoyed the most. Still, she obeyed. Her son's behavior settled down after that. She knew she had made the right decision, though it was difficult.

God sometimes even shows his purposes when we are willing to acknowledge that his agenda is more important than our own personal peace and prosperity, when we are willing to follow him wherever he will take us. After the period of my husband's job struggles, I wanted to put it all behind me. But I began to sense that God wanted me to write about it. To do so would open old wounds for both Gene and me. But the Holy Spirit patiently kept bringing to mind other people who were struggling through the same thing, and feeling alone in their pain. At the same time I felt a stronger impression that I was to write about what we had learned. Finally I wrote an article. The article won an award. And the sense that I was to expand it to a book increased. When I obeyed, God showed me from his Word that this was one way he would redeem Gene's and my experience, that it was for the good of others that he allowed us to go through the fire.

Openness. This is related to humility. It is an attitude of openness to whatever God may do or ask of us, and a receptivity to however he may choose to speak. It follows humility. In humility we say, "God, do with me whatever you want." Then we are open to listening and looking for how he will answer that prayer.

Of course we need some spiritual discernment at this point. If we believe God is telling us something that contradicts his Word, it is not from God. A woman who was dating an unbeliever prayed that God would show her what to do. She felt he was telling her that she could go ahead and marry him. She felt he was giving her a promise that the man would come to know God. I am skeptical of this "message" from God, because it contradicts the clear scriptural command not to be yoked with an unbeliever. After great struggle, she decided not to marry him. If he became a believer, she would give him time to grow and establish himself in the faith before she married him. She received confirmation from other Christians for this course of action, and her confusion melted away.

Discipline. Another word would be focus. If we are to hear God, we must make it a priority. We must tune in. We must take some time; we must keep coming back to the goal: to keep in touch with the living God on a daily basis.

This isn't always easy. As a mother of a preschooler and a newborn, I know! I don't always have time for much Bible study, but I'm finding the most important thing is focus. When I consciously turn my thoughts to God, even if it's just for a moment to acknowledge my need for his help, his patience, his strength, I find he is there. I have found it helpful to simply say to myself, in my mind, a single word: "Jesus" or "Lord" throughout the day. It is a way of refocusing, of turning toward God. It reminds me that he is here with me, as he promised. It tunes me to look for his grace in each day. The more I train myself to do this, the easier and more automatic it becomes.

Obedience. When God speaks, we need to respond. If we don't, our hearing becomes dull. Of course, outright sin cuts off our communication with God. But so does not responding in the smaller matters: A friend comes to mind, and you wonder why. It was probably the Holy Spirit bringing that person to mind for prayer. If you don't pray, then you desensitize yourself to those inner promptings of the Spirit.

I often get impulses and intuitions. No doubt not all of these come from God, but I have learned to bring every one of them before God in prayer, asking what if anything I am to do. Then he either makes the impression stronger, or it disappears. For a long time, however, I mistrusted such inner promptings. They stopped. And something seemed missing from my walk with God.

Eventually, they started up again. This time I began to listen, and pray, and respond if there was no scriptural reason not to. And God has continued to use this means in my life.

He may use other means with you. The point is, if you don't feel God has been speaking to you much lately, think over your past. Were there times you felt he was speaking, and you didn't respond? Ask him for forgiveness for those times. Ask him to quicken your hearing. Then, listen up!

Telling others. A willingness to share God's work in your life with others is also important. Not always, but probably more often than not, when God gives us something or does something wonderful for us, we are to tell others about it. He is not only out to bless us. A friend just called me today to share some quotes from writing conferences that were especially helpful to her. Her sharing them with me blessed me, and came as a word of encouragement that ultimately, I believe, was from God.

Frank Laubach was a missionary to India who brought literacy to thousands. During the year of 1937, he kept a journal in which he tried to capture daily the messages God was giving him, through any source whatsoever. As he did so, he became more and more impressed that the messages were not for him alone. He wrote: "I must talk to others about You more than I have done. I can neither help them nor discover their deepest best unless I reveal this fellowship with You to everybody. To meet You every minute of every day and to share You with others is to live a full life."[1]

Sharing your experiences of God will not only bless others and show them how God works, but it will confirm the experience in your own heart. It may be difficult to do at first; proceed slowly, praying for courage to share. Start with your closest relationships, with people who also are open to God. I have found such sharing pulls me closer to other people, as well as to God.

Faith and trust. This is the most important key to seeing and hearing God. Trust that you will recognize his voice, for he promises it (John 10:3–5). Trust that he desires to commune with you. Trust that he is always at work in your life, that he is good and he knows what's best as he leads you.

My friend Pat, a single mother of three young children, went through a difficult divorce. Yet she is full of joy and the strength of God. She says that through all the turmoil of the marriage breakup, she had an underlying sense that something good would come from everything. "I don't need sympathy because there's more to all this than the circumstances," she says. She can recount many, many instances of God providing encouragement through a friend, money for Christmas presents, comfort when she was most fearful, strength when she was weakest. Through it all she has come to know and trust and love God as never before. No, she says, don't feel sorry for me. For I have seen God at work, and none of the trials compares to the wonder of that.

If, as Frank Laubach and my friend Pat have discovered, fullness of life consists of this daily sense of God's presence, how do we tune in? In the next chapter we'll look at several ways.

Chapter Eight

How to Tune In to God

I received in the mail an advertisement for a device that, when plugged into an electrical outlet, will purportedly "turn your whole electrical system into a giant television antenna," thereby greatly boosting reception. I don't know if it works. But it reminds me of the fact that the signals are out there, in the air. What determines whether we receive them crisply on our television screen is the equipment on the receiving end.

Tuning in to God is like that. God's messages, his gifts, his grace, are all readily available. He isn't holding back—his Word and my experience tells me he is ever present, wanting to make himself known. Whether I receive what he's sending has much to do with me. So let's look at what we can do to tune in to God.

TAKE THE TIME

The first step to tuning in to God's messages is to, in effect, switch on your receiver. It means to deliberately turn your focus to God in the morning, and consciously invite him into every corner of your life for that day. Ask him to open your eyes to his work in your life. Then, read something from the Word, to give God

some material to work with. He may or may not use that particular verse or passage that day, but I have found the continual
input of the Word opens me up to God, and he brings it back to
me when I need it. Also, continually bathing yourself in Scripture
sets that filter in place, so that during the day you can filter out
what is not from God.

It doesn't necessarily take a large chunk of time to tune in.
Some of us simply don't have that. I don't, at this stage in my life,
when I am raising small children. Sometimes the input has to be
"fast food" because there is no time to sauté a gourmet meal.
Here's what I do: I keep a magazine holder in the bathroom, and
in it I put my Bible, a notebook, a devotional, and any other book
or magazine of a spiritual nature that I may be reading at the
moment. I take a few moments each morning to either read a
chapter from the Bible, or a section from the devotional. I pray
that God would open my eyes to what he wants to show me, I
read, I pray. Sometimes I have a moment to jot down a thought,
a prayer, or a dream. Whenever I can at other times in the day—
when my son is taking a bath, for instance, I may pick up the
Bible or book. It may be "fast food," but I find that it is better than
starvation. God uses it; it is my way of turning on the receiver at
this stage of my life.

Of course, taking time to listen for God in solitude and
silence is also important. I sometimes do this late at night. It is
difficult, in our busy, noisy, complicated world to find time to just
be silent before the Lord. I have noticed that even so-called
"retreats" are often filled with an agenda rather than time to be
alone and still before God. It is a constant battle, but I am convinced we need to simplify our lives as much as possible so that
there are wide margins where God can write his messages.

LOOK TO YOUR PAST

One key to understanding God's love language to you, as
we've seen, is in your past. How did he speak to you, as noted in

your spiritual autobiography? Start to pay special attention to those means now.

But realize also that your circumstances may have changed. God is always at work, ever doing new things. The more open you are to him, the more he will speak through a variety of means.

Look To Your Present Circumstances

Another way to tune in to God is to look at the circumstances of your life. Pray for an openness to hear him, and begin to pay attention. He may use your job, your children, your relationships, books, times of prayer and preparation—any number of things. Expect him to speak through the circumstances he's already called you to.

My work has always been a source of God's input. Sometimes it's through a devotional guide I am preparing; God seems to speak to me even as I try to teach others. Or I interview someone, and their story of God's work in their lives gives me exactly the encouragement I need in a trial of my own. Or I come across a book that turns out to be very important to what God is showing me at that time.

Do you teach a Sunday school class? Does God use those lessons you prepare in your own life? If not, perhaps you aren't listening.

Many parents find that God teaches them as they try to parent their own children. A friend who I believe has a gift for evangelism says God speaks most clearly to her through the questions and searching of her seeking friends. Someone else who leads Bible studies comments on how amazed she is that she seems to need those particular Scriptures at that particular time.

If your circumstances frustrate you because they seem incompatible with hearing God, pray about it. Perhaps your own preset expectations are blocking out God's messages. I felt this way for a time about giving up my job to be home with children. I felt frustrated at the lack of time to spend with God. But as I prayed about it, I realized that if God has called me to this task for now, he would continue to speak to me through it. And he has. I just had to set aside my expectations and learn to see him at work in new ways.

LOOK TO YOUR STRENGTHS

If God works and communicates to us as individuals, it's often in terms of the natural strengths and preferences he's built into us.

I have found it particularly helpful to understand psychological type theory in this regard. This theory is based on Swiss psychologist Carl Jung's observation of the different way people's minds work as they relate to the outer world. His theory was further developed by Katharine Briggs and her daughter, Isabel Myers, over a period of nearly forty years. Basically, the theory says that everyone was born with innate preferences in four main areas:[1]

1. Where you focus your attention and get your energy (extroversion or introversion)
2. What information you trust the most (senses or intuition)
3. How you make your decisions and judgments (logic or personal values)
4. How you like to structure your life (with an emphasis on the perceiving function or the judging function)

As you use and develop your innate preferences, you develop a distinct way of relating to the world. I believe this predisposes you toward certain paths of spirituality as well. The four preferences make up sixteen different combinations, or "types." Briggs and Myers researched and documented these combinations of traits and developed the *Myers-Briggs Type Indicator* (MBTI)®.*

Since the MBTI is a tool used in many settings, from business to churches, you may well already know your type. If not, you may want to find someone in your area who can administer

---

*MBTI and *Myers-Briggs Type Indicator* are registered trademarks of Consulting Psychologists Press, Inc.

the MBTI. If your pastor or a local counseling center can't help you, contact the Association of Psychological Type (APT), 9140 Ward Parkway, Kansas, MO 64114, (816) 444–3500 for a list of people in your area who can administer the MBTI. Costs to take the MBTI vary, depending on the setting and purpose.

As part of my research for this book, I did an informal survey of a couple of dozen people, asking them questions both about their spiritual walk and about their type preferences. Usually there was a correlation between the two.

Extroverts tend to be attuned to the outer world and get their energy from people and the outer world. They usually get more out of group interactions: corporate worship, small groups that meet for fellowship, prayer or Bible study, committee work. In contrast, those with a preference for Introversion tend to be attracted to solitude, reflection, and meditation. They get their energy—and tend to feel they meet God best—when they have time alone for personal reflection.

In the second category of preference—Sensing or Intuition—those with a sensing preference tend to find God best through singing or hearing songs and hymns, by expressing themselves through movement, or creating something. Sensing people trust and focus on what comes to them from the senses. Intuitives, on the other hand, look for patterns and possibilities and trust their "sixth sense." They would report that God spoke to them through their intuition, through inner dialog, through dreams, through patterns they saw in circumstances or their own lives, and through stories—either in Scripture or the testimonies of other people.

Interestingly, both Sensing and Intuitive types spoke of the importance of nature. But they approached it differently, true to their different types. Sensing people focused on letting their senses soak up the experience of being in nature itself. They observed what was around them and found themselves refreshed by the encounter—an encounter they felt was somehow connected to experiencing God himself.

Intuitives looked at nature as a metaphor for deeper truths. As Sanna Baker said, "Everything in nature is a metaphor." Poet Luci Shaw, another Intuitive, believes that "everything points to something else—there are correspondences on different levels." It is the particular gift of the poet, I think, to make these connections and help the rest of us to see the deeper meanings that are present in the world. But Intuitives also need Sensing people to help them experience the joy and wonder of the experience itself. I know from my own life that we Intuitives can get so caught up in the connections and possibilities that we can miss the experience itself.

The next set of preferences—Thinking and Feeling—also affect the way we experience God. Those who prefer Thinking tend to take a more logical, objective approach to reality. This spills over into their spirituality: They will tend to encounter God through reason. They like to wrestle with understanding theological concepts but may be more concerned with understanding them on an abstract level than with applying them to their lives. Feeling people encounter God not through abstract concepts but through relationships. It's not enough for Feelers to understand a theological truth intellectually; they want to know how to apply it. Prayer, indeed, everything about their spirituality, will have a feeling component. They will need to somehow "feel" God's presence.

I have been in Bible study groups that were dominated by the Thinking approach. Being Feelers, my husband and I often felt frustrated by the seeming lack of desire to apply what we were learning into our daily lives. Understanding the difference between preferences has helped us realize we need both approaches. Thinkers help Feelers to focus on what a passage is actually saying. Feelers challenge Thinkers to wrestle with how the passage relates to real life.

Finally, the fourth pair of preferences corresponds to whether we like to approach life—and our spirituality—in a structured or spontaneous way. Judgers prefer structure and plans. They are the ones who have their regular "quiet times" and follow a set pattern. They may get a lot out of structured reading or Bible study guides; some I know keep a detailed prayer list, praying for certain things on certain days. The danger for Judging types is that they may tend to "control" God, or may close off his voice because they only expect him to speak in certain ways or at certain times. However, their strength is that they do tend to develop the discipline to regularly take time for God.

Perceivers, on the other hand, feel boxed in by too much structure. They look for God any time and everywhere. They feel comfortable praying when some need or person comes to mind, rather than at set times. The danger, of course, in this approach is that they may never get around to prayer, or Bible reading. They need discipline to round out their spiritual life.

Knowing your preferences in these areas can help you be more open not only to how God may work with you naturally, but also to those areas where you need more balance. For instance, my preferences are Introversion, Intuition, Feeling, and Perceiving. (In type terms, that makes me INFP.) As an Introvert, I nurture my relationship with God primarily through reflection and solitude. But I also need people, and find God speaking to me often through others. If I depended on that primarily, however, I would soon feel "out of touch" with God. While I need people for balance, I have to make time for solitude and reflection a priority.

As an Intuitive and a Feeler, I find God communicating to me often through inner impressions and promptings. I have found I can trust these, more often than not; it is God working through my natural preferences. However, I also need to make sure such subjective impressions are confirmed by more objective realities. I need to check things out against Scripture, and other believers whose opinions I trust (especially believers who have strong "common sense"—usually a Senser). For instance, it wasn't enough to just "feel" that Gene was the right person for me. Wisdom suggested that I look at more objective criteria: Was he a believer, were our values and goals compatible? In my career, I have largely let my heart guide me ("do what you love"). But I also take into account objective realities, such as our financial and family needs. And finally, as a Perceiver, I tend to value spontaneity. But I know that unless I set up some structure in my work and spiritual life, I quickly flounder. Taking time to focus on God every morning, however briefly, and to plan my day start me in a direction. I am open to God moving me in a new direction as the day progresses, but at least I have a place to start.

As you reflect upon, pray about and pay attention to the ways God seems to speak to you, keep in mind your natural preferences. If you've been feeling dry and boxed in with your spirituality, it could be that your church or your background has shaped you in a way that is not natural to you. Begin to experiment with other forms of openness to God.

For instance, if you have been brought up to be very structured in your quiet times, try a new approach. Choose one of your favorite passages and just meditate on that throughout your day. Ask God to open your eyes to ways he's working in other areas of your life.

Or perhaps you grew up with an emphasis on always being around people and on service. If your bent is toward introversion, this may prove taxing. Allow yourself some alone times of prayer and meditation, perhaps out in a natural setting, and see what happens.

Listening and Looking for God

In the midst of your circumstances, and as you explore your own natural preferences, prayerfully listen and look for God. I have found it helpful, in discerning how God might be at work in my life, to look at some of the following areas.

Key questions. Ask yourself: What are the key questions I have about God/life/myself right now? Take them to God in prayer and ask him to open your eyes to his answers.

Key Scriptures. Is there any Scripture that comes to mind over and over? Meditate on it. Ask God to keep showing you what it means.

A verse that comes to me often these days is Proverbs 14:1. I have taken this verse as the guiding principle for this season of my life, but as I meditate on it God is ever showing me fresh ways to apply it.

Key images. Sometimes, for some of us, an image comes to us as we pray. One friend, after filing for a divorce, couldn't get out of her mind the image of coming out of a cave. As she thought about this image, she realized that the cave had been her marriage—a place of darkness and lies. The image helped her trust that even though she never wanted that divorce, God was freeing her from this cave and she would be living in the light.

Sometimes dreams recur to us that the Holy Spirit highlights as important. I don't think that dreams are God's normal way of communicating, but they can be one way. If God wants to show us something through a dream, the Spirit will make it clear.

A dream was instrumental in my coming to the Lord. I had been looking into Eastern philosophy in my search for God. But God in those systems is an impersonal force. One night I had a dream that impressed me at the time as being important somehow. In the dream, I was camping with my family, but I got lost. As I wandered through the darkness, scared, I came upon a man sitting on a bench, under a lamplight. Somehow I was drawn to him. I sat on the bench and he engaged me in conversation. Before I knew it, I was pouring my heart out to this person. I knew he understood me better than anyone else in the world. And then he hugged me, and I awoke with the most wonderful feeling of peace that I have ever felt, even to this day.

I knew at the time that the dream was important because of that feeling of peace. As I kept remembering the dream, I slowly realized that I was looking for the source of that peace, and that the source must be a person, not a force. Eventually, as a friend shared the gospel of Jesus with me, I realized that I was lost in the dark, that Jesus was the person in my dream, the person who understood me better than anyone and loved me and wanted to give me that peace I felt. I came to Christ and knew that the dream was fulfilled. The imagery in the dream (darkness, light, a God who understands and loves and is the source of peace) was scriptural, so I feel that the dream was indeed one of God's ways of communicating to me even before I really knew him.

If you have a dream that somehow seems out of the ordinary, pray that God would show you what it means. Confirm whatever it is you think he's telling you through Scripture or a wise counselor or prayer.

Service. Are you involved in an area of ministry or service that God seems to be blessing? Look not only at how God is using you to help others, but how he wants to speak to you as you serve. For instance, parenting is a ministry that yields many rich lessons of how God himself parents us—lessons in forgiveness, unconditional love, the importance of discipline.

Circumstances that don't seem to change may be God's messenger. I've already shared how God has been using my present house to teach me about frugality, his provision, simplicity, contentment, and the value of being organized. If there are any circumstances that really loom large in your life, ask God what he wants to show you through them.

Other times circumstances seem so serendipitous we start to pay attention. My friend Grace suddenly kept bumping into a certain person whom she hadn't seen for many months previously. She began to feel she was supposed to spend some time with that person. Finally she called and suggested they go for a walk together. At the time Grace was agonizing over whether to leave her mentally ill husband. Determined not to mention her situation to this woman—Grace felt she would be judged—somehow the topic came up in the last few blocks of their walk. The woman stopped Grace and said, "You would be so right to leave. My father had the same illness, and my mother never left." The woman then poured out her story of the pain that resulted for her whole family.

To Grace, that encounter was from God. She needed all the encouragement she could get to leave her marriage, because leaving went against everything she believed was right. Still, in this situation it seemed that God was clearly trying to tell her the marriage was destructive and it was time to get out.

Relationships can be God's instruments, as we've seen. Expect God to work through your close relationships, both positive and negative, and even through more casual encounters.

Once you have a sense of the means God tends to use to speak to you, deliberately include those things in your life. It may be certain books or speakers, music, people, keeping a journal, certain ways to take in Scripture, a particular Christian radio program. The means are different for different people. God meets us where we are, shows us what we need to know of him, and beckons us to new territory.

And often that territory takes us into our own weaknesses, where we glimpse a whole new aspect of God.

Chapter Nine

Mapping Your
Spiritual Development

Mary Beth's life was together. She had three children and a husband who loved her. She had realized her dream of being a successful journalist and was writing regularly for several prestigious national magazines and newspapers. The articles she often wrote—inspiring stories of people doing good deeds—gave her a sense of mission and purpose. Involvement in her church grounded her spiritually. She felt strong, she was ministering to others through her gifts. She was blessed.

But then tragedy struck. Her neighbor was hit by a car right in front of Mary Beth's house, and she witnessed his death. She was pulled into the high-stakes world of personal injury litigation as a witness. The case dragged on for years as insurance companies wrangled over whether there would be an insurance settlement for the widow and surviving child. Mary Beth was forbidden to talk to her neighbor or the child at all during those years; she had no way to express her caring and sympathy and concern for a widow who herself had been disabled the year before from a car accident, and had no way to earn her own living.

Other incidents that year showed Mary Beth something that changed her forever: She was not as strong as she thought. The trial was a nightmare in itself, requiring her to relive the horror of seeing her neighbor splattered on the sidewalk, the confusion of trying to help the woman driver whose car struck the man, and the ache of not being able to reach out to her neighbor. To get through the trial, she was forced to reach out to other people. That proved emotionally scary, because it exposed another truth about herself she had never faced. She vividly recalls the first time she confessed to her pastor her realization that she kept people away by trying to be perfect. "He was the first person I admitted any weakness or need to," she says.

But that confession became the stepping stone of a new era of growth for Mary Beth. "Before, when I was always trying to be so strong, I wasn't real," she now says. "Now, if I have a need, or I can't help someone, I just express the truth."

Some people couldn't handle seeing Mary Beth step off the pedestal. Others were there to support her. Most of all, God was there. He was there in the people who cared for and accepted her at her weakest. He was there in her church's worship, he was there during her prayer times, which suddenly were nothing less than a lifeline for her. She sensed his presence in the new opportunities to serve, to care for others who were scared or depressed or hurting.

Through facing her own weaknesses, Mary Beth opened herself up to new dimensions in her experience of God's care and character. And so it is for all of us. If God often speaks to us through our strengths, he *works in us* through our weaknesses.

The Many Faces of Weakness

What do I mean by weaknesses? Sometimes they're our strengths taken too far. One of Mary Beth's strengths was caring for others. But during her year of painful revelation about herself, Mary Beth realized that she overused this strength until it became a liability. Her caring had evolved into always being the strong and giving one. People came to depend on her to be that, and that alone. Eventually such "strength" hardened into a wall that kept people from really knowing or caring for her in return.

Weakness is what we feel during times of trial or stress or illness. In the face of difficult circumstances, we realize our fragility and inability to control life.

Weakness also takes the form of character flaws, wrong patterns of thinking, bad habits, sinful behavior patterns. Together our weaknesses make up what the Bible refers to as "the flesh." It is that part of us that is out of alignment with Christ's image in us. God wants to correct that. The wonder is that he does so in a supremely gentle and loving way.

WHAT GOD DOES THROUGH WEAKNESS

God comes to us in a unique way when we are weak. "For this is what the high and lofty One says—he who lives forever, whose name is holy: 'I live in a high and holy place, but also with him who is contrite and lowly in spirit, to revive the spirit of the lowly and to revive the heart of the contrite'" (Isaiah 57:15). I love this verse. The high and holy One comes to live with the person who admits to his or her own weakness and need! He revives us spiritually and emotionally, doing some of his greatest work toward making us like Jesus Christ.

For that is his purpose: to conform us to the image of Christ, according to Romans 8:29. He gives us the creation gifts of our strengths, through which he uses us to serve him. But he uses our weaknesses to glorify himself in a number of ways.

Our weakness forces us to acknowledge our need of God. Before I came to Christ for salvation as a teenager, I tried very hard to "be good." I remember going through each day, concentrating very hard on not doing or saying something wrong. Every day I failed, in some big or little way.

My most valiant attempts at righteousness were utter failures. That fact more than anything convinced me I needed God.

Weakness enables us to depend on God. Whenever I face a task that feels too immense for me to handle in my own strength—

whenever I am weak—that is when I lean most heavily on God. And he always comes through! We've already seen how God uses trials and tough circumstances to help us trust in him. During our times of weakness God delights in coming to us in his strength. That's because *he's* the one who gets the glory, not us.

I'm always encouraged by the story of Gideon in the Old Testament. When God came to Gideon, Gideon couldn't believe it. God told him he would defeat the Midianites who had crushed Gideon's people. Gideon responded, "Who, me? How can I save Israel? My clan is the weakest in the group, and I'm the least in my own family." But God told him to go. Gideon gathered some men to help him, but God whittled them down to three hundred men, armed only with trumpets and torches encased in jars. With this motley crew, God defeated the Midianites and the Israelites reclaimed their land. (See Judges 7–8.)

This Old Testament story is a wonderful illustration of Zechariah 4:6: "'Not by might nor by power, but by my Spirit,' says the Lord Almighty." God longs to show the world the wonders only he can do. When we allow him to do this in our individual lives—and we also give him the credit—he becomes real not only to us but to the world.

Weakness deepens our experience of God's sufficiency. The apostle Paul had some kind of affliction, a "thorn in the flesh," that he prayed fervently for God to take away. God did not take it away. But he did tell Paul, "My grace is sufficient for you, for my power is made perfect in weakness" (2 Corinthians 12:9). That changed Paul's perspective on his weakness, to the point where he could "boast about" and "delight in" his weaknesses, "for when I am weak, then I am strong" (verses 9–10).

When we are weak, we depend on God. Then he comes through for us, and we experience his power and sufficiency—*personally.* Mary Beth calls her year of trials "the scariest and sweetest of my life." The uncertainty and pain threw her into a new dependence on God, and the experience of him catching her and sustaining and carrying her through sweetened the experience.

It is during weaknesses and trials that we learn the truth that "neither death nor life, neither angels nor demons, neither the present nor the future, nor any powers, neither height nor depth, nor anything else in all creation, will be able to separate us from the love of God that is in Christ Jesus our Lord" (Romans 8:38–39).

Weakness enables us to understand grace. When we truly face the depths of our own sinfulness, and at the same time grasp the forgiveness, cleansing and healing that God offers, the result is not self-condemnation but a sense of wonder at God's grace. I don't believe we can fully appreciate the marvelous gift of God's forgiveness and complete acceptance of us until we face the depths of our sinfulness. I know Christians with low self-esteem who, fearful of feeling worse about themselves, try to gloss over their weaknesses and sins as signs that they're "only human." But I don't think that approach truly frees us. Until we fully comprehend our own dark depths, we can't grasp the amazing fact that God knows even those parts of us and loves us anyway. We will always in some sense spend energy trying to hide those dark parts from ourselves, from others and from God.

I remember a time when this truth vividly hit home. When I was in college, I had a close friend who found herself pregnant. Her mother was forcing her to get an abortion. The thing that bothered me the most was that the mother professed to be a Christian, and had been helpful to me in my Christian walk. How could a so-called Christian coerce her own daughter into snuffing out an innocent life? Oh, she had her rationalizations. She seemed to firmly believe that because the baby's father had abused drugs, the baby would be deformed. That was her defense.

I railed against her and my friend to God. Anger, sorrow, indignation, helpless rage spilled out of me in prayer as I walked the campus. But slowly, something happened to me. I realized that had I been in that situation—young, afraid, pregnant, abandoned by the father of the baby—I might allow myself to be swayed into a wrong choice. If I were a mother to whom a pregnant daughter would be one of the worst disgraces—that is how I believe this woman felt—then I too might find myself rationalizing my behavior.

In fact, by the end of my prayer time, I realized that I myself was perfectly capable of these same sins. Then I pondered the fact that even now, even when the terrible deed was being done, God stood ready to offer these people forgiveness. He was forgiving me of my judgmental attitude. God's grace broke through the terrible darkness of that moment of anguish. That is what I remember best from that terrible incident.

Facing our own sins and weaknesses is never easy. We should never attempt it without God's help, and often the presence of another believer who understands grace and forgiveness. We bring our sins, our weaknesses, to the foot of the cross, where Christ suffered the full penalty for us, and we leave it all there. When we do this, we receive forgiveness and cleansing by faith. Even if we don't feel it right away, we claim it as ours because God promised it.

First John 1:8–10 shows us how the dynamic works: "If we claim to be without sin, we deceive ourselves and the truth is not in us. If we confess our sins, he is faithful and just and will forgive us our sins, and purify us from all unrighteousness. If we claim we have not sinned, we make him out to be a liar and his word has no place in our lives." Denying our weaknesses and sins doesn't make them go away; it just embroils us in a lifestyle of self-deception. It cuts us off from both truth and grace. But confessing our dark side—agreeing with God about what's there and what it means—results in forgiveness and cleansing. We become free from sin and from guilt.

This is the heart of the good news. God wants to make it experientially real as we acknowledge and entrust him with our weaknesses.

Weaknesses produce humility. Just as I realized that I was, in fact, no better than my friend who got the abortion or my friend's mother, facing our weaknesses produces humility. When we fully realize that even our strengths can twist into liabilities, we understand that apart from Christ and his work in our lives we can do nothing.

Weaknesses link us to the body of Christ, to other believers. Not only do we realize we need God, but we need to lean on the strengths of other people as well. If I can't balance my checkbook for beans, I have to depend on my husband to make up my lack. When a church event needs to be planned, I depend on those with better organization skills than I to make sure nothing falls between the cracks.

Humbly accepting our own limitations pulls us into relationships with others whose strengths are our weaknesses. First, however, we have to admit we have a need or a limitation or a struggle.

This is not always easy. We want others to see us as capable, strong. But I have seen over and over what God can do when we admit a weakness appropriately. For instance, when I admitted to a friend certain struggles I was experiencing in trying to love my husband, she told me that she was convicted to pray more about her own marriage. I was encouraged that my confession helped her; we both ended up praising God for the wonder of how he works through each other and through our weaknesses.

Weaknesses produce compassion. Mary Beth said that because of her experiences, she now understands and empathizes with people who experience depression or fear. Since my husband's employment struggles, both he and I are very sensitive to anyone who is undergoing stressful times, and we try to reach out. I've also noticed that when we share our own struggles with others, it frees them to be more open about what's real in their lives.

God uses our weaknesses to encourage others. People who "have been there" offer unique comfort to others who suffer in similar ways. The countless support groups for everything from facing cancer to conquering addictions to dealing with the loss of a child prove that there is healing when we reach out to others in the same kind of pain. Pain, suffering—weakness—can bond people in a common search for comfort and meaning and hope.

Weaknesses allow God to work toward balance and wholeness in our personalities. Any of the personality preferences mentioned in the last chapter—extroversion, introversion, sensing, intuition, thinking, feeling, judging and perceiving—carries with it a complementary weakness. Extroverts need to develop their capacity for reflection, Introverts the ability to act on what they know. Sensing people may lack vision and get caught up in particulars, while Intuitives overlook important details. Thinkers often need the balance of warmth and passion in their spiritual lives; Feelers must ground their enthusiasm in solid doctrine. Judgers need spontaneity for balance, while Perceivers struggle with discipline. Part of the balance is found in Christian community. But we are also to seek balance within our own personalities.

When we become aware of our limitations and needs and turn them over to God, we allow him to work on all these things. But it's difficult to face ourselves as we are.

FINDING BALANCE

Some of us see only our weaknesses, not our strengths. We berate ourselves for what we are not. But even though we seem to see our failures most clearly, we do not deal with them as God would like. Unless we entrust them to God, we can remain stuck in old patterns. We need to believe that our weaknesses are part of us, that God has a plan for them as well as for our strengths, that he can use them in mighty ways if we give them to him.

Others of us spend a lot of energy trying to deny or overcome our weaknesses on our own. Usually we're not aware of this attempt. I fall more into this category. I have had to face the fact that too often I keep myself busy with worthwhile endeavors to keep from facing the darker side of myself. I subconsciously try to prove to myself and others that I have conquered my problems, that I have it "together." I feel uncomfortable having needs or admitting to weaknesses.

But I'm learning. I understand that my shame at having needs or being weak comes not from God, but from a background distorted by false beliefs. I am finding that when I face my darker side and give my weaknesses to God, he gets to work. He really does! For instance, when I have a problem I pray or write about it in my journal. And often, God shows me my part of the problem. I may start out feeling frustrated at some deficiency I see in my husband, and by the time I've prayed or written about it, God has shown me my contribution. Yet he does it in such a gentle way, I am able to face it and confess it.

When the Holy Spirit convicts us of sin, he does so not with a sledgehammer but with a velvet-gloved finger. Like an expert doctor, he places his probing finger on the weak spot and makes it hurt just enough for us to identify the problem. Then he says, "Okay, we agree on the problem. Now I'm the surgeon, I'll take care of it."

It's not our part to change ourselves; only God can do that. It is our part to be open to him, to confess our weaknesses, to submit ourselves to his surgery. Unlike the world, God doesn't think less of us when we admit to our weakness. He welcomes us with an open heart: "The sacrifices of God are a broken spirit; a broken and contrite heart, O God, you will not despise" (Psalm 51:17).

Much of our spiritual development depends on what we do about our weaknesses. To map a course that God can use, here are some suggestions.

MAPPING YOUR SPIRITUAL DEVELOPMENT

First, let me stress that only God can direct the course of your spiritual growth. He alone knows best where you need to start. He alone knows your needs. He alone knows how your strengths and weaknesses fit into his big plan.

So, relax as you go through this process. These suggestions are meant to help you put yourself in a place where you can perceive God's working in your life and cooperate with him. Let him lead you through the process.

Step One: Pray. This is always the first, middle and last step toward God. Prayer is at the heart of a life with God. When we pray, we acknowledge our need of God. We ask for direction. We listen. We admit our ambivalence about obeying. We face our own fears. When we add meditation on God's Word to our prayer, we readjust our thinking so that God's thoughts become our own.

When you pray about facing your weaknesses, ask the Holy Spirit to reveal the truth. Ask him to show you what you need to work on, how to handle what he shows you, what each step should be. When something does surface that needs to be confessed, name it for what it is (fear, unbelief, selfishness, greed, whatever). Ask for a sense of forgiveness. Ask God to help you realize what you're doing the next time you do it.

Seek in expectation that he will show you, step by step, and gently.

A word of caution: As you start this process, you might feel fearful that God will show you more than you can handle. He never will. If you begin to feel plagued by guilt or dark thoughts, these are not from God but Satan, the accuser of souls.

Search God's Word for promises and comfort. Pray for protection from the evil one. If the problem persists, talk to someone. Do not make the mistake of attributing torturous thoughts to God. The ways of the Holy Spirit are "love, joy, peace, patience, kindness, goodness, faithfulness, gentleness and self-control" (Galatians 5:22). When he convicts sin, there is a brief pain of guilt, but it is always accompanied by the release of forgiveness. I have found that he always gives me the strength to face what he shows me, when it is through the Holy Spirit. And he will confirm something either through his Word, through circumstances, or through other believers.

Step Two: List your strengths. Remember that our strengths can easily become our liabilities. Once you've got your list, submit it to God. You might want to write a letter to God asking him to take all of these and do with them what he will. Ask God to show you which, if any, have become unbalanced.

In the following days, if God reveals anything to you, write it down. Begin to notice the times he gives you opportunities to make a different response.

To give you an example from my own life: One of my strengths is that I am action-oriented. If there is a problem, I pray about it, do what I can to fix it, and leave the rest up to God. I am not a worrier.

This orientation usually works for me. I can even find lots of verses to back it up. Lately, however, God seems to be showing me that there are situations where my response is not loving. When someone shares a problem with me, my first inclination is to kick into my problem-solving mode. I offer lots of great advice and perspective. At least, I'm convinced it is! Sometimes the other person is, too, but there is still something missing. I believe the Holy Spirit is teaching me that it is usually better for me to just listen to the other person. To offer advice only when asked, even if I think I have the solution. To let the Holy Spirit guide that person, not me.

Once God revealed this to me, it seemed he gave me opportunities to practice a new response several times a week. Sometimes I chose my old pattern, sometimes I didn't. When I chose the path the Holy Spirit seemed to be forging, I had an inner sense that God was pleased, that I was making progress.

Step Three: List your weaknesses. Again, focus only on those things the Holy Spirit brings to mind readily. Don't dig too deep or try to be exhaustive. God will add to your list in his own time and way. He knows what you can handle at this time. He doesn't want to beat you up.

Some possibilities might include: the flip side of your strengths (as opposed to the overuse of your strengths); a bad habit or attitude; a wrong perspective; a particular area you find it difficult to trust God about; a relationship that is troublesome; a character defect such as lying or stinginess or greed; emotions that seem to dominate you, such as fear or mistrust or anger or lust.

Step Four: Look at ways you've already grown. Ask God to show you areas that used to be weaknesses, areas he has used to help you grow, or to encourage others, or to make you more humble or dependent on him or aware of his grace.

Thank him for his work in your life in these areas. Let the truth of his grace and his reality seep into you. He is at work in you, and here is some evidence! Be encouraged.

Step Five: Pinpoint areas for growth. Let God do this for you as you entrust your lists to God. You might want to picture yourself going to Jesus and handing him your lists. Say something like, "Please take these and do what you want with them."

Ask God to show you one or two—no more than three—areas which he wants to use. Picture him taking a highlighter and marking what he wants you to work on. It may be from either your list of strengths gone awry, your list of weaknesses, or areas of growth that still need attention.

Step Six: Explore avenues of growth. Again, come to God for direction. Ask him to reveal the best means for developing in the chosen area for growth. I'll give you some possibilities. Some of the following methods may attract you naturally; perhaps God has used them in the past to help you grow. He may continue to use them in the future to refashion your weak areas. But the method itself may encourage growth and balance in new directions. Consider this as you prayerfully read the following suggestions.

Read. Find good authors who have a biblical perspective on your problem. For those who are linguistically inclined, this is often a very good choice. It's also a good discipline for those who need to slow down, or develop their inner life.

Reading widely is the best way to expose yourself to those authors who seem to speak to your unique concerns. I have found several authors of fiction and nonfiction whose writing seldom fails to inspire me: Madeleine L'Engle, Gordon MacDonald, Francine Rivers, Philip Yancey, Richard Foster, Luci Shaw, to name just a few.

Devotional Classics, edited by Richard Foster and James Bryan Smith, has proven to be a gold mine of spiritual insights. It is a good introduction to a number of men and women throughout the ages who have wrestled with spiritual issues. Some of them that I particularly resonate with, such as John of the Cross or Madame Guyon, I have investigated further.

Keep a journal. "God seems to speak to me whenever I pick up a pencil," says Martha. There is something about keeping a journal that tunes us in to our inner life, and opens us up to listen to God. It also helps us face ourselves. Somehow most of us feel freer to write the truth than to speak it. That's why this discipline is ideal for anyone who feels a need to develop the inner life, or whose weakness is of a more private bent. God may also use it for those who have a natural inclination toward reflection and writing.

Your journal is what you want to make of it. Ask God to help you be very honest and free with it.

Go on retreat. This may be a natural for people whose bent is introversion, but extroverts may need it even more. Retreats are ideal times to interrupt your daily business and focus on God.

Join a small group. If one of your weaknesses is failure to make significant connections with people or otherwise being in more meaningful fellowship, this method may take courage. But it's worth it.

As an Introvert, I naturally gravitate to one on one relationships. I always disliked groups. At the same time, I was lonely. I sensed God leading me to join a small group in my church. Though it was difficult at first, I stuck with it. God used that experience to help me grow in many ways. Ironically, now I am in three small groups! Each one gives me something different, and in each one I contribute something different.

Seek a spiritual mentor and/or prayer partner. Perhaps your approach has been too broad, and you sense God leading you to meet with someone who will hold you accountable for growth. A spiritual mentor is someone who is more mature spiritually, someone who is willing to disciple you. A prayer partner may be more of a peer. Either kind of relationship can provide someone to encourage you on your journey.

Find a way to serve. This avenue is especially useful for moving you out of your comfort zone if you're overly inclined toward reflection or analysis rather than action, or if you're caught up in your own problems, or if you've simply become too selfish. It's possible to become unbalanced even in one's search for spiritual growth—we can spend all our time trying to grow, and in the process neglect the needs of those around us!

Look to the classical spiritual disciplines. Over the centuries, Christians have adopted certain spiritual disciplines to put themselves in the way of growth. It can be very fruitful to use these patterns in your own spiritual development.

Dallas Willard, in *The Spirit of the Disciplines*, breaks some of the classical disciplines into "disciplines of abstinence" (solitude, silence, fasting, frugality, chastity, secrecy, and sacrifice) and "disciplines of engagement" (study, worship, celebration, service, prayer, fellowship, confession, submission).[1]

In *Celebration of Discipline*, Richard Foster focuses on a slightly different list, which he breaks down into "the inward disciplines" (meditation, prayer, fasting, study), "the outward disciplines" (simplicity, solitude, submission, service), and "the corporate disciplines" (confession, worship, guidance, celebration).

James Bryan Smith takes a different approach in *A Spiritual Formation Workbook*. He looks at five dimensions of the spiritual life that historical Christianity has emphasized through the ages: the contemplative tradition, the holiness tradition, the charismatic tradition, the social justice tradition, the evangelical tradition. Each of these "streams" of Christianity offers unique insights into the nature of God and Christian discipleship. All of them can be found in the life of Christ. So, a balanced spirituality will seek to include perspectives from each dimension.

Just looking at these lists and categories may stimulate your thoughts of where you might need the most growth. These books, along with other resources you may find when you start looking, can guide you through the process.

Share your struggle with another person. Sometimes the best way to deal with a sin or weakness is to tell someone else what you're going through. That person may be God's messenger of

comfort and encouragement to you. Or, you may find that sharing your burden helps the other person to open up, or face a sin,
and that helps you to see God's purpose in your own suffering. If
you sense a prompting to reveal something, and it seems appropriate, go ahead, even if you feel uncomfortable. Sometimes our
problems shrink when we bring them out to the light.

Learning the language of God means grasping what he
wants to do through both our strengths and our weaknesses. Both
come from him; both are usable to him. As we offer our whole
selves to God, we will find him doing two things: he will conform
us to the likeness of Christ, and he will shape us for unique service to other people.

It is to this second aspect that we now turn: how we can
respond to God's initiative through service. The more we learn his
"love language" to us, the more we can understand how to love
him in our own "language."

Chapter Ten

LOVING GOD
IN YOUR OWN LANGUAGE

On Mother's Day, our church sponsored a special recital in which many of the children either sang or played a special musical selection for their mothers. One piece struck me as particularly poignant. Not because of the musician's virtuosity. In fact, the young violinist playing A. Thomas' Gavotte from *Mignon* stumbled and screeched through the piece. The mistakes grated, but somehow, amid all the wrong notes, I could make out the melody. The look of concentration on the girl's face bespoke her effort. And it was an effort of love, an offering of her time and talent to her mother, who herself was a gifted musician. When the girl finished and beamed at her mother and bowed, it struck me that her playing was truly beautiful. What made it beautiful was the love with which it was offered, the effort that went into it.

This image lingers in my mind as I think of our response to God. As we seek to serve and follow him, it's our love, our passion for him, and our effort I think he sees. It doesn't matter whether we present a flawless performance or not. Our best effort, given in love, delights God's heart.

When we truly grasp God's love for us—and especially when we begin to experience that personalized form that whispers to us in the particulars of our circumstances and strengths and weaknesses—we desire to love him back. His love for us calls us to respond. We are not simply to be the receivers; he desires a relationship, and relationships must be mutual. God woos us because he covets our love.

But how do we love God? God loves us in a general way—by giving us his Son, and the Holy Spirit—and in particular ways—through the Holy Spirit's ongoing activity in our lives. Made in his image, we can also love God in a universal and an individual way.

The universal way—the response to which every Christian is called—is obedience to his Word. "If you love me, you will obey what I command," Jesus said (John 14:15). Jesus gave many commands, but they all boil down to what he called the two greatest commandments: Love the Lord your God with all your heart and with all your soul and with all your mind, and your neighbor as yourself (Matthew 22:37–38).

Obedience enlarges us to receive more of God. I have taken to looking for the good things God gives me each day, and jotting them down in a journal. I have noticed on the days when I have paid particular attention to giving loving rather than irritated responses to my children or husband, God has been more real to me and I have discovered more ways he has worked.

Praise and adoration also open us to God. For instance, I don't always feel like attending church, but I almost always go anyway because he deserves my praise and worship. When I sing praises to God and hear his Word expounded, invariably he speaks to me in one way or another.

Our obedience in the particulars of life, our praise, our service to others form the individualized way we respond to God. As we love God in the particular context of our own circumstances, strengths and weaknesses, we in a sense create our own love language of response.

RAINBOW REFLECTIONS OF GOD'S LIGHT

Jesus declared, "You are the light of the world" (Matthew 5:14). John and James talk about God being light, with no darkness dimming it. Paul said as we look into God's face, we reflect his glory (2 Corinthians 3:18), his light.

The interesting thing about light, as I understand it, is that when it comes from the sun, it is pure white light, containing all the colors of the spectrum. But as it strikes certain objects, those objects will absorb some of the colors of the spectrum and reflect other colors (or combinations). So, grass absorbs all the colors except green; it reflects green, and that is why it looks green to us. The particular hue an object will reflect is built into its molecular structure, created into its nature.

To me, these characteristics of light and color are a rich metaphor for our own love language. God created our unique nature, gave us specific backgrounds and circumstances, and through these we reflect some of the aspects of his light. Each of us has, if you will, a unique "color" or hue to reflect to the world. This is our love language to God.

PRAYER, WORSHIP, AND WORK

This love language of response has three interrelated components: prayer, worship, and service or work.

Prayer is the opening up of ourselves to God. It is the presenting of our needs, the expression of our feelings, the longing of the heart for God. It is also listening for God. Prayer is one of the most personal ways of responding to God. And God urges us to "pray continually" (1 Thessalonians 5:17). To do so is to maintain an inner attitude of openness to God in whatever we are doing. In a way, everything we have talked about in this book is about prayer—that attitude of listening for and to God in whatever way he chooses to speak to us in any given moment.

Worship is also the natural response to being gripped by God's love. In worship we acknowledge God's great worth. We praise him for who he is. We sit in simple adoration at his feet.

And we offer him back everything he has given us—body, mind, and spirit. Some of us worship with our voice, or through a musical instrument. Others embody our deepest spiritual expression through movement, in sacred dance. All of us do it in one form or another in our relationships with other people.

Worship then takes on yet another aspect: service, or work. We place who we are, our very uniqueness, on the altar as a gift. Our worship inevitably spills out into a tangible form of service to others, for we cannot love God apart from relating to others. God made us not to be little islands emitting praise to him, but a community as intimately related to each other as parts of the body are to the whole body. He also intends his followers to be witnesses in the world of his greatness, mercy, and love to sinners.

These are his general goals for each follower. Our job is to discover the specific ways we can do these things. I think of this as fashioning a particular life response that reflects our own uniqueness and the special ways God has revealed himself to us. It is like creating our own special love "song"—and I think it's a song that thrills him just as the young girl's violin composition thrilled her mother.

How do we begin to fashion a personal life response to God?

LOOK TO YOUR GIFTS

One way is to look to our gifts. Many of us feel we do not have any gifts, because we look for the spectacular. Our culture exalts the superstars; the rest of us can feel insignificant by comparison.

The Bible says that all of us have gifts. Those who have studied intelligence, or who work with people to help them identify their natural abilities, confirm that everyone has a number of natural gifts. Because this is an area that has always fascinated me, I have done much research on the different ways of understanding innate abilities. And I have found that different people approach it in different ways. To me, this speaks of the rich diversity God has built into each one of us.

Looking at lists might help you identify some of your natural, God-given abilities. In Richard Bolles' best-selling *What Color Is Your Parachute?* he lists 250 skills as verbs and also identifies numerous transferable skills. Thomas Armstrong, in *7 Kinds of Smart*, lists ways to determine whether you have linguistic, spatial, bodily-kinesthetic, musical, logical-mathematical, interpersonal or intrapersonal "intelligence." Other approaches key off of personality type.[1]

The Bible itself contains lists of gifts: prophesying, serving, teaching, encouraging, contributing to the needs of others, leading, showing mercy (Romans 12:6–8); also working miracles, healing, helping, administering, speaking in tongues (1 Corinthians 12:28). But these biblical lists are not exhaustive. Other passages throughout the Bible illustrate that people may have creative gifts, musical gifts, craftsmanship, interpersonal gifts, gifts of persuasion, preaching and more. The main point the Bible stresses about gifts is that they are to be used for God's glory and the good of God's people. Your gifts are not to be enjoyed by you alone, but employed for God's purposes. That is how they become your gift back to God, your main expression of his goodness to you.

Because God's gifts are expressions first of his grace and particular love for each one of us, and because we express love to God by offering our gifts back to him, I believe it's well worth our time and effort to discover and develop these aspects of our uniqueness. If you don't already have a sense of your innate giftedness, I urge you to begin to discover your gifts today.

Here are some suggestions, based on my research and personal experience.

Step One: Pray. Again, the first thing is to seek God's guidance in the whole process. Pray with assurance: God certainly does want you to discover your gifts and use them for his glory. Would a parent buy a special gift for a child and then hide it so well that the child never finds it? The whole point, the joy for the giver, is having the recipient open the gift and seeing the look of joy that says, "What a fantastic gift! Thank you!"

Step Two: Ponder past joys. Make a list of things, big or small, that you have done at any time in your life that gave you satisfaction and joy. Don't look only for the things other people recognized as "achievements." In fact, pay particular attention to the things you used to enjoy doing as a child. When we're young, we have the most freedom to engage in things that naturally attract us. These are wonderful clues to those seeds of greatness God has planted in each of us.

A friend of mine has a special gift for staging special events, from conceptualization to planning the details to executing the event. Hope uses this skill professionally—she runs focus groups for businesses—but also to minister to others informally. For instance, she may host a baby or wedding shower. She plans special experiences that will make memories for her children. She invites her child's teacher over for a special dinner. These are some of her ways of loving God with her gift.

When Hope recalled some of her early satisfying experiences, she discovered that one of her earliest experiences was making something special for someone: At age seven she made some sock babies for her new little brother, using scraps from her grandmother's sewing basket. At age twelve, she planned and coordinated a surprise party for her parents' twenty-fifth anniversary. These activities were freely chosen and deeply satisfying to her.

As you recall your past experiences, look for things you did that gave you particular joy in the doing. After you've jotted down brief descriptions of everything that comes to mind along these lines, pick seven to ten of your favorites.

Step Three: Expand on your joys. Once you've whittled down your list to your favorites, find a way to describe in detail exactly what you did, how you did it, why you did it, and what gave you satisfaction. You may write out your stories, you may talk them into a recorder, you may tell them to someone who will take notes and tape the interview.

The advantage of the latter approach is you will get someone else's feedback. This is often invaluable, since we often overlook our natural abilities simply because they feel so natural to us. It's not until someone points out, "I wouldn't have been comfortable talking to a stranger like you did" or "I'm not naturally that organized" that you begin to realize not everyone can do certain things as easily as you can. If you choose this approach, just make sure that the person is able to simply listen first in a nonjudgmental way. While you tell your story, that person's main job is to listen and elicit details in these four areas: what you did, how you did it, why you did it, and what gave you satisfaction.

Hope described how she planned her parents' anniversary party: "Somehow I got it in my head that it would be good to remember their anniversary. I planned it down to every detail, delegating things to people. My brother and sister cleaned the house; I contacted a woman from my church to make the cake; I bought pretty white invitations and mailed them to some close friends and relatives. On the day itself, my boyfriend and I took my parents out to dinner. They hadn't a clue about the party. When we walked into the house, everyone popped out and yelled, 'Surprise!' I've never seen my parents treated so nicely by people.

"The satisfying parts were thinking up the idea, planning the details, getting other people to cooperate, and pulling everything off. It was a special time for all who came. But most fulfilling was giving my parents a very special gift—not a thing, but an experience."

Step Four. Look for patterns. Go through your stories and look for recurring themes in those four areas. Were you always trying to do the same kind of thing (for instance, befriend someone, or create something, or help someone)? Did you usually take a certain approach (seek people to help you get the job done, work alone, pioneer a situation, find someone else to work with)? Were you often motivated by the same result (to come up with a tangible product, to persuade, to learn, to compete)? What gave you satisfaction (performing, discovering, creating, connecting with people)?

As Hope looked at her other satisfying experiences, again and again she noticed that she was often creating either something tangible (a sock baby) or an experience (the anniversary party), and that she used skills such as visualizing, creating, organizing, coordinating or arranging, and supervising.

The patterns you pinpoint in your experiences are the building blocks for your unique service to God. They are what I call "energized abilities," because when we use them we feel energized, alive, at our best. Who else would have given them to us but the Lord of Life?

Step Five: Confirm your gifts. Ask other people what they see as your gifts. Some abilities you may already have developed to a high level, and they are obvious to other people. Other natural talents may be more dormant. Ask God for opportunities to use and develop your gifts. Experiment. Build on what you've already done, no matter how small. Seek opportunities to develop them, especially in the context of building up other Christians through them.

I recall one woman who realized she always loved to write, but never thought she could actually get published. She began small, keeping a journal and writing for her church's newsletter. As she offered her writing ability to God, opportunities to learn more about writing and publishing opened up. She pursued them, step by step. And eventually, she did become a published author. None of that would have happened if she hadn't offered her gift to God and asked him to do what he would with it.

God will also show you avenues you should not bother pursuing. I remember getting very fired up about photography at one point. I took a course in it, practiced, considered photojournalism as a career direction. I offered this up to God, asking him either to confirm it or change my direction. He changed my direction. I now realize that I am not naturally oriented to the visual; I am much more aurally inclined. I was glad I asked God early on to guide my exploration in this area, before I wasted a lot of time and effort.

Step Five: Give priority to your gifts. Develop them. Pray for more opportunities to use them. Begin to fashion your life around them.

For instance, one of my energized abilities is writing. I have organized my life around this in many ways. I write to earn money for my family. I try to keep a journal to facilitate spiritual and personal growth. I record our family life, the funny or cute or insightful things my children do and say, the things that are important to our life as a family. Someday my children will be able to read these accounts and get a flavor of their early life, at least from their mother's perspective.

I use writing to serve the community as well. I write a column for the national newsletter of a mothering group in which I am active. I try to write brief notes of encouragement to friends and family.

Writing has become a major component of my "love language" to God as I use it to serve him. For others it may be music, or dance, or making things, or fixing things, or encouraging others, or nurturing children, or teaching, or . . . the list is as endless as the number of possible gifts and combinations of gifts God has given to human beings.

God, I'm convinced, delights in them all. Anything done for love of God warms his heart.

LOOK TO YOUR PASSION

Another way to discover and express your love to God in a personal way is to focus on a passion you may have. Perhaps there is something you really want to do in the world. You have always wanted to do it. Maybe you haven't yet had the opportunity, but the dream is still there. Pray about it. Ask God to open up opportunities, if this passion really is from him.

Or perhaps there is some cause or need that really moves you. Something about child abuse causes profound grief in me. Someday I would like to do something positive to stem the terrible tide of innocent children being scarred for life. At this point in my life, the positive thing God seems to have put before me is raising my own children with love and compassion, and sharing love with any other children God puts in my path. Perhaps in the future, there will be more I can do.

Your passion may rise out of a problem you have overcome. Many wonderful ministries have been started by people who have seen God work in a mighty way in their own lives, and they want to reach out to help others in similar circumstances. Joni Earickson Tada allowed God to use her terrible accident to develop a ministry to handicapped people, and sensitize others to the needs of handicapped people and the ways God can use tragedy for good.

I've seen people stifle their passion and bury their gifts because they don't see any way to express them. I believe this is a mistake. Offer it all up to God, and let him flame it or bury it as he sees fit.

Look to Your Circumstances

Even if you don't know your gifts or your passion, you have a great starting point—your circumstances.

Start with where you are. God has already put people into your life to serve. If you are married, you serve your spouse. If you are a parent, you also have daily opportunities to serve your children in a myriad of ways. Everything you do—wash dishes, fix meals, stoop down to listen to a preschooler's story—if done with love, may be planting a seed that will bear fruit years later. Remember Ernest Boyer's strong recollection of his grandfather crouching down to listen to him and really look at him? Boyer never forgot what it showed him of love, even God's love, to have his grandfather so tenderly attend to him.

Boyer also recalls the example of a woman named Sarah. One thing Sarah knew how to do and could do, in her circumstances, was bake bread. That simple ability became her expression of love to God and others. She baked dozens of loaves at a time, all to be given away: to churches for their fundraising; to soup kitchens; to her family; to neighbors who needed some extra care or for anyone else she heard of who needed help.

"'God tells us to give what we have,' she would say. "All I have to give is my bread.' But as Boyer points out, "She was giving much more than that. She was giving a special kind of love, a love that at once reached out to others while also making her life all of one piece, so that everything she did, routine or ordinary as it might otherwise seem, came to express that love."[2]

Perhaps you're in a position where you cannot realize your dreams or utilize your gifts as fully as you would like. Sometimes God puts us through a time of waiting on those things. But he has not forgotten us. He has put us in a place and time when there are opportunities at hand to serve and express our love to God. As we do so, he takes the ordinary and blesses it. Jesus said, "If anyone gives even a cup of cold water to one of these little ones because he is my disciple, I tell you the truth, he will certainly not lose his reward" (Matthew 10:42).

Poet Sanna Anderson Baker expresses this idea well in her poem, "Ordinary Loaves and Fishes." The poem opens with her lying beside her child, singing the hymn "Great Is Thy Faithfulness." She meditates on the wonderful and often mysterious ways God proved his faithfulness through the centuries of redemption history. Then she concludes with this prayer:

> And now, as your strange ways would have it,
> the Spirit that is you has come to me
> and I, not ark, bear you through the world.
> Bearer of your image, I? I do no miracles—
> make no manna, sight no blind eyes.
> I tie laces, make beds, bake bread.
> But your equations, like your ways, are strange
> adding oil, multiplying meal, making one lunch
> food for thousands. Take my acts,
> ordinary loaves and fishes.
> Bless, break, multiply.[3]

Ernest Boyer calls service through the ordinary acts of family living "life in the center," and believes that family life is itself a spiritual discipline. Boyer calls the offering of our mundane acts of service in the ordinary business of life "the sacrament of the routine." As we offer up our ordinary acts in a spirit of love and worship to God, God transforms the everyday until we see his hand even there.

The more you ponder and try to live this truth, the more exciting it will become. As Boyer says, "To find this awareness of the presence of God in each moment of your life is to discover the secret of the sacred within the ordinary, which is the heart of the sacrament of the routine. . . . You come to sense some powerful force at the center of all that is, a force at once infinite in majesty, while also small and intimate—vaster than the universe itself and as close to you as the beating of your own heart."[4]

Unusual circumstances may also be an opportunity for service and the unique expression of our faith and love. I have a friend who is battling cancer. Her continuing faith in God, the opportunities she has seized for sharing her faith, the loving way she has deepened her relationships with family and friends have touched many people. In the face of very trying circumstances, her unwavering faith is a poem more eloquent than she has ever penned, accomplished writer though she is.

This triad that is given to each one of us—a unique set of gifts, a unique passion, and unique circumstances—form the "grammar" of our love language to God. When we respond to him by offering each of these to him, and following as he leads us in the paths of service laid out by our triad, we compose a poem that uniquely expresses our love to him.

But sometimes it takes courage to do so. And always it requires faith.

THE COURAGE TO SPEAK YOUR LANGUAGE

It may take courage to speak your language to God.

The first reason is that people may misunderstand. As you hone your gifts, as you fan the flames of your passion, or as you seek to contentedly serve God in ordinary or extraordinary circumstances, other people may intentionally or unintentionally block your path. You may feel judged for what you're *not* doing even as you seek to do what you think God wants you to do.

For instance, the woman who leaves her job to stay home with young children may be charged with "wasting her education." In other circles, the mother who continues to use her gifts in a work setting would be judged as a "bad mother." A man who refuses a promotion because it would mean uprooting his family, or because he believes his gifts are best used where he is, is also opening himself to possible ridicule. Someone who focuses on a passion—for instance, to save the unborn by opposing abortion—may be dismissed as "unbalanced."

Then too, our obedience to God's calling—for that is what serving him comes down to, a sense that *this* is primarily how we are to give back to God—sometimes proves costly to others. Because we are involved in God's overall purposes, our obedience affects others. We must first make sure we are perceiving God's call accurately before we subject others to the cost. But if we are sure, we must obey and trust that God will take care of those who are also affected.

Evangelist Ravi Zacharias was called to a ministry of evangelism that required he be away from his family a good deal of the time, traveling, as the children were growing up. Though it was hard for him and for the family, he attests to the way God has kept his wife and his family in his care, and shown them ways to mitigate his absence. Today his children feel they are a part of his ministry and that they are all serving the Lord together.

Finally, it takes courage to speak your language to God because there will always be a great measure of faith required for the response he asks of you. "The kind of assignments God gives in the Bible are always God-sized. They are always beyond what people can do because He wants to demonstrate His nature, His strength, His provision, and His kindness to His people and to a watching world."[5] Remember that God may do more through your weaknesses than through your strengths. The point is always that God gets the glory, not us.

KEEP THE RELATIONSHIP PRIMARY

Our love-gift to God is the use of whatever he has given us, wherever he has put us, for his purposes and his glory. It should always be a response to the love we have experienced in our lives, not a means of earning his favor. Therefore, if you ever find your service turning into mere duty, so that it is no longer your love-song to the Lord, take time to rekindle the flame of your passion for God. Remember that Jesus told the church in Laodicea that their lukewarmness nauseated him (Revelation 3:16). He rebuked the church in Ephesus for forsaking their first love for him (Revelation 2:4).

Keep the flames of your fire for God burning, and make that your first priority. I know of no other way to do that than to constantly fill your mind with the truth about God from his Word, to open yourself to whatever he is doing in your life and however he is asking you to respond, to look for him and his work in your life and in the world.

Then stand back and be ready for some surprises, because God's way is always bigger, fuller, richer, broader, and deeper than we ever expect.

Chapter Eleven

OPEN TO GOD, OPEN TO OTHERS, OPEN TO GROWTH

The other day for the first time, I heard a real lion roar. My husband, son and I were at the zoo on a cool, cloudy June day. When we got to the lion cage, the two lions were snoozing. After admiring the hugeness of the lions, the majesty of their manes, we walked around the outdoor cage, looking for tigers in the next cage. Suddenly, one of the male lions got up, padded a few yards over to a rock, and proceeded to roar. Again and again.

We stood about sixty yards away, but the sound filled the area. It was a mighty sound. The lion started low, and got louder and louder. It roared for maybe two minutes while we stood transfixed. Afterward, the lion trotted back to its napping spot and resumed its rest.

I kept thinking of Aslan in C. S. Lewis' *The Chronicles of Narnia*. Lewis chose a lion, Aslan, to portray what Christ would be like in a place like Narnia, where animals can talk and trees take on human-like forms and dance. In one scene from *Prince Caspian*, the children are trying to decide the best way to get to Prince Caspian. Suddenly Aslan appears, but only Lucy sees him. He appears to be beckoning them to go the exact opposite way than their reason told them was correct. Lucy insists it is Aslan, and that they must follow, but nobody believes her. They take a vote and decide to go their own way, the way their past experience and reason tell them is right. Eventually they discover that their reason led them astray; they are almost killed by their enemies in the process.

Aslan again appears to Lucy. He seems bigger to her than when she'd last seen him. Aslan explains it's because she is older, that the more she grows, the bigger he will seem to her. Lucy and the others get a second chance to follow Aslan. Lucy is still the only one who can see him. Edmund takes her side and follows, out of "blind faith" at first, but soon he too can see Aslan clearly. And so the others, Peter and Susan, and even the ever-skeptical, practical-minded dwarf Trumpkin, see Aslan as they obey and follow.

Then they come to their destination, the Great Mound, Aslan's How. And Aslan roars. "The sound, deep and throbbing at first like an organ beginning on a low note, rose and became louder, and then far louder again, till the earth and air were shaking with it. It rose up from that hill and floated across all Narnia."[1] The roar started a great Romp in the wood—a joyful, dance-like celebration in which trees and vines and donkey and mythological creatures all expressed their overflowing joy in their own ways.

When the Lion roars in our own lives—when God is on the move—we must expect the unexpected. We must be ready to abandon reason at times in order to follow God's way, as Lucy, Edmund, Susan and Peter from the Narnia Chronicles discovered.

God is personal, yes. In this book we have explored many dimensions of that. He comes to us as he comes to all his children—through nature, through the Word, through the Church. He reveals himself intimately in our individual lives through the Holy Spirit, who uses our uniqueness—both gifts and weaknesses—to enable us to perceive God's work in our lives and to serve him. But God is also majestic, and beyond our understanding. God will always resist our labels and expectations. As one of the Narnian characters said of Aslan, God is not "tame."

Just when we think we have him figured out, he does something totally unintelligible. Just when we think we know where to go, he beckons us in the opposite direction. Just when we feel okay about ourselves, and start to depend on our own strength, we fall flat on our faces. And in humility we ask God to forgive and pick us up again, and we find he is still there, forgiving us seventy times seven and more.

ADVENTURE, JOURNEY, AND DANCE

Life with God is always an adventure. It may involve pain—but then we find him transforming the pain into something glorious. It may include doubt—and even as we question, we find God drawing us deeper into himself for answers. It may lead us through the valley of loneliness—only to discover that God was by our side each step of the way. It usually entails tedium—but as we embrace the ordinary givens of life, somehow we begin to find God there too, teaching us to love, to trust, to give, to pray, or to hope.

Life with God is a journey—into ever new dimensions of God. It will take us all of eternity to explore all of God. In this life we are always searching, always on the way, always prone to stumbling and falling. We long for something, for home. We try to make this world our home, but it never feels quite right. That's because we were made for our true home, heaven—the place where God is. Our journey does not end until we come home to God.

Life with God is a dance, a dance of intimacy that changes as he changes the music. He leads, we follow. Swept away in his arms, we dance together through life. But in this dance, I have noticed that there are three basic movements—with endless variations on each movement. Each dance, like a ballet, tells the story of our life with God. Each is unique, but there are several "themes" that run through every story.

GOD PURSUES US

The first movement, the first "theme" in the story of the soul's life with God, is his pursuit of us.

God is always the one who seeks us first. If we begin to search for him, we eventually realize it is he who has awakened our soul's hunger. When he meets us, he meets us wherever we are.

In the children's story, *The Runaway Bunny* by Margaret Wise Brown, the little bunny tells his mother he will run away. The mother bunny says if he does, she will run after him. The little bunny says if she runs after him, he will become a fish in a stream and will swim away from her. She responds, "If you become a fish in a trout stream, I will become a fisherman and will fish for you." The bunny then says if she does that, he will become a rock on the mountain, high above her. She says if he does that, she will become a mountain climber, and climb to where he is. And so on, through all sorts of transformations. No matter what way the little bunny thinks of to hide or run away, the mother comes up with a way to find him. The little bunny finally concludes that he might just as well stay where he is and be her little bunny.

To me, this story beautifully expresses the kind of love God has for us. No matter how we try to hide from or run away from him, he finds a way to pursue us, for we belong to him and he longs for each of us to dwell with him.

When God pursues us, he shows us himself as the answer to our need. When I came to Christ, as I mentioned earlier, I was seeking someone who knew me, understood me, and loved me thoroughly. I found that in Christ. He always meets us where we are and reveals whatever aspect of himself is balm to our particular wound. He may have to reveal his stern side and cut out a cancerous tumor first. But just as Christ went about healing while on earth, so God's ultimate purpose is for our wholeness.

He reveals himself as the answer to our present need—but then he moves us on. He wants us to know more of him. This theme of our running and God's pursuit is clear in a conversion experience. But in a subtler way, it is an ongoing process. At least in my own life, I can think of plenty of times I try to "run away" or hide from God. For instance, when he puts a finger on a sin, a sin that I have struggled with for years, I find myself suddenly getting very busy. It seems at those times I find lots to do—work, see friends, organize my house, even go to lots of religious meetings. But then something happens and I find he's still there, trying to show me how to deal with that same old sin. He hasn't moved; he's been waiting patiently. I've been the one running, hiding. He throws some people or circumstances or Scriptures my way to catch my attention. And finally I turn to him and say okay to his surgery, and perhaps we make some progress toward cutting the cancerous tumor out of my life.

God may pursue us through any number of means, in order to reveal to us what he wants us to know of him at any particular time. God pursues us, not just to bring us to Christ once and for all, but to keep us close. This step of our flight, his pursuit, and reunion is part of the dance that recurs all through the ballet of our lives.

WE DIE TO THE OLD

Another movement in our dance with God, another theme of the ballet, is death. We can't escape it. Though Christ died for our sins, once and for all, death is an integral part of intimacy with God. Christ told us that in order to follow him, we would have to take up our cross daily and follow him (Luke 9:23). The cross was the place where Jesus was crucified. It is the place where we die to the old in order to open ourselves to the new, to resurrection. Paul the apostle elaborated on this truth he seemed to know well. In fact, the longing of his life seemed to be "to know Christ and the power of his resurrection and the fellowship of sharing in his sufferings, becoming like him in his death, and so, somehow, to attain to the resurrection from the dead" (Philippians 3:10–11).

This experience of death in Christ and resurrection life seemed to be something that can be experienced in this life; in Galatians Paul said he has been "crucified with Christ," that it was no longer he who lived, but Christ who lived in him. The life he lives in the body, he explains, he lives by faith in the Son of God, who loved him and gave himself for him (Galatians 2:20).

God will ask us to die in any number of ways. The general biblical theme is that we die to our sinful nature. But what does that entail? For each of us it is something different, perhaps. To one it may be compulsive habits, to another anger, to another fearfulness. Since all of our nature—physical, intellectual, spiritual, emotional, relational—is affected by this tendency to go our own way and the destructive results, "death" may occur on any number of levels.

On the deepest level, though, I think the death God calls us to is the death of our distorted views of God. In reading the story of Aaron and the golden calf, I am struck by how quickly the Israelites, who had just witnessed great miracles of God's power, nevertheless fell into idolatry. In the last few months I have been reading through the Old Testament history of the kings of Israel and Judah. Over and over I have been struck by the litany of the kings who trusted not in the Lord, but in their own power and might or in their alliances with other kings. Other kings fell into idolatry. It seems a very ingrained part of the sin impulse to make for ourselves gods we can control, gods we can understand, rather than submit to the true God who made heaven and earth and has absolute moral authority over our lives.

Several years ago I wrote an article about the New Age movement. I really liked the title Jim Long, one of the editors, came up with: "Small God Inside." It was, I think, an apt description for a belief system that basically says, "God is whatever you want to think of him as."

That charge fits the New Age movement. But I think it's also easy for believers to fall into the trap of thinking inadequate thoughts about God. As J. I. Packer says in *Knowing God*, "This is where most of us go astray. Our thoughts of God are not great enough; we fail to reckon with the reality of his limitless wisdom and power. Because we ourselves are limited and weak, we imagine that at some points God is too, and find it hard to believe that he is not. We think of God as too much like what we are."[2]

God says himself he is a jealous God. The biblical books of prophecy show the great lengths to which he will go to destroy his people's distorted views of who he really is. Much of the pain in my own life has entailed, on the deepest level, the death of my own false view of God.

For instance, financial stress has uncovered how much I would rather trust in a growing bank account than in the God who provides. Conflicts with my husband are often caused by my own need to control—in essence, to act as God in my own and even my family's life. I might want to point to times from the past when I suffered from other people's shortcomings as an excuse for my behavior, but God doesn't allow that. He calls me to trust that he can and will deal in his own time and way with other people's shortcomings, and even help me if I suffer because of other people's sins.

I read in the New Testament that greed is idolatry. Jesus said we cannot serve God and Money, we cannot both seek the kingdom of God and chase after our own security and comfort. Following the one true God entails the pain and death of crucifixion. Jesus was crucified for our sins. We become "like him in his death" as we are willing to die to the old patterns that alienate us from God. Those patterns are unique to each of us, but the need to die to them is part of the universal dance.

I doubt that we'll ever be finished with this phase, either, until we die our physical death and are finally home. There will always be new areas of alienation that God points out. Just as God cuts out the disease from one area, it crops up in another.

Another aspect of dying to self occurs as we deny ourselves and do our duty in the ordinary tedium of life. Commuting day after day to a job that offers little satisfaction, or tending to the endless needs of children and household demands—these feel like a death of sorts. The dreams of greatness we cherished in our youth dim, and we face the fact that we are ordinary mortals destined for no earthly greatness. Even those who do attain some level of recognition in terms of the world's standards can point to someone greater. King Solomon, perhaps the richest, wisest and greatest man ever to live, said all such achievements are in themselves meaningless.

Death is the dance movement that feels wooden. We go through the paces, feeling little joy, perhaps feeling as if we dance alone. But each time there is a death in some area, we become ready for the next and glorious step: resurrection—awakening to the new. Anyone who is willing to share in Christ's crucifixion is also privileged to share in the greatest miracle of all—new life after death. We may not feel it, but we are dancing right into the arms of our Partner.

EMBRACING THE NEW

Whatever we allow God to put to death in us, that he will also transform into something new, something full of life. Jesus said he came to bring us life, life in all its fullness (John 10:10). It is no less than the resurrection life that he experienced after his own crucifixion. It is life on a totally new plane.

What does this new life look like?

First of all, it is a life that longs for God. There is an appetite to know God, to understand what he wants, to desire what he wants. We seek God, and as we seek, we begin to find more and more of him. We begin to know his ways.

And as we learn his steps, we trust him more. Become more abandoned to him. This is the part of the dance where we are closest to God, where we follow effortlessly, breathlessly and with great joy as he leads. We hear the music, we are one with the music and our partner, our feet feel light.

On the resurrection plane, we are open to however God will speak to us. We begin to find God anywhere when we expect him to be everywhere. We no longer seek to confine him in a box, to keep him tame, but we allow him to be and do whatever he wants. We truly believe he is at work in our lives and in the world, and we begin to look for him everywhere. Perhaps this is part of what it means to "fear the Lord." When we really allow God to be

God, to do whatever he wants with us, whether that entails pain or suffering or joy, we feel a stab of fear. We don't want to feel pain, we don't want to suffer. But allowing God to be God means trusting him even if that's what he brings. And as we cultivate this attitude, we start to see God more clearly in our lives.

It is also a life of discernment. We begin to understand the difference between God and the means he uses to communicate. God may often use intuition as part of his "love language" to lead me, but God is not my intuition. My intuition may lead me astray. Through prayer and a searching of the Scriptures I need to hone my ability to discern when it is God speaking through my intuition and when it is not. We rejoice in and enjoy the gifts, and any and all means of revelation, but we keep in mind that he is greater than any and all of these things.

So along with longing for God, openness to God, and discernment, the resurrection life includes humility. We do not try to make our own experience normative for others. Nor do we accept the experience of other people, no matter how insightful, as normative for us. One person feels freshest in the morning, and so insists that morning time is the best time to meet with God for everyone. He or she may even give a string of very convincing reasons why this must be true for all. But this leaves a new mother, who is often up several times a night with her infant, feeling guilty because she doesn't take time to get up before the rest of her household to have a "quiet time." I say we need to be careful about making what works for us the norm for all Christians. Believe me, as a writer who seeks to teach others, this can get tricky! But all I can and should do is share what God is doing in my own life, and let God use that as he wills in the lives of other people.

As we dance the resurrection steps with God, our lives take on a new character that shines for others. It is holiness, Christlikeness. We, if we are truly in step with God, won't notice it ourselves. We're too busy looking into the Master's face. But some of his glory, his character, shines from him onto us, and others notice it. And so, through us, they too begin to see something of God.

Finally, when we dance with God, we start to notice that other people are also dancing with him. This dance is not ours alone. We are part of a great cosmic production. We each have our own steps, our own part, but our part interweaves with the parts of others in a much greater show.

OPENNESS TO OTHERS

And so we develop an appreciation and openness for the unique ways God works in other people's lives. Just because my way is not your way, that does not mean that you haven't heard something from God that I, too, need to hear. An appreciation of God's kaleidoscope of revelation should make us more appreciative of the fact that God reveals a little bit of himself to each of us. To get the full, big picture of God, I need the insights he reveals to others as well—especially others who are very different from me.

I have several friends who deeply believe in God, but the specifics of their belief vary from mine. One is from another denomination. Her God is very concerned with service and with community. From her I learn more about these aspects of God, which my own church expresses a bit differently. Another friend has one of the deepest thirsts for God and the deepest spirituality of anyone I know. She has not found the God of the Bible, but as we compare notes about God, I glimpse how he is dealing with one woman's thirst. I do not try to tell her that she is pursuing the wrong God. How do I know that the true God isn't leading her along her own path to him? What I do is share my own experience, and why I think the Bible is so important to understanding who God is. And I pray for her, for only the Holy Spirit knows exactly how to draw her to the truth.

Another woman I know has experienced much suffering: an unbelieving husband and extended family who mocks her faith, two wayward children, a battle with cancer. She continually tells people, believers or not, that God will work everything out. It is tempting to think of her faith as a crutch, to believe that in the guise of faith she is denying reality. But I received a card from her recently, and God does seem to be working miracles. Dare I call her faith "denial"? Can I call myself a believer and not believe, with her, that God can redeem even the life of someone who has embraced drugs and promiscuity?

OF CHILDREN AND SHEEP

To know God, Jesus said, we have to become like little children. Open to all life has to offer, open to seeing things in new ways. One of the things that delights me so about my four-year-old son is his ability to see an object in many different ways. A hooded towel is his "cape" (either Batman's or Superman's). His names for dinosaurs are descriptive and straightforward: Tyrannosaurus Rex is "sharp tooth," Stegosaurus is "sharp tail," and so on. He prays for everything—for the car to start on a cold winter's day, for me to find the plug to his wading pool, for Daddy's headache to go away. And more often than not, his simple prayers are answered. If they aren't, at least not right away, he will say insistently, "But I prayed about it." Yes, he does need to learn that God is not a genie that will always do our bidding. But his implicit faith that God cares about what's important to him, and that he will answer without a doubt, are aspects of faith that I think Christ had in mind.

It all comes down to knowing the Master's voice. Jesus said he is the Good Shepherd who lays his life down for the sheep. His sheep know his voice, and they follow him. They know him by his voice. The voice is tender in our moments of great need and weakness; stern and sorrowful over our sin; warm and gentle with forgiveness; steady when we stumble in darkness; loud and majestic when we feel too important. Hearing the tone, straining to listen to the exact words, and then responding—this is what it means to have a personal relationship with the living God.

"He who has an ear, let him hear what the Spirit says...."

Discussion Guide

Though each person's journey with God is an individual one, many of us benefit from sharing our experiences with others. Also—and perhaps more importantly—someone else's experience or insight may be what God uses to encourage, exhort, or otherwise stimulate our own spiritual growth in some way. Therefore it may be useful to go through this book with another individual or a small group who shares a desire to experience more of God.

The questions below are designed to stimulate discussion among a group that has read each chapter. They may also be used as a catalyst for keeping a journal or for one-on-one discussion with a partner in your spiritual growth. The "action step" suggestions will help you incorporate some of the concepts presented into your daily experience.

Introduction: A Hunger for God

1. How connected to God do you feel at this point in your life? On what do you base your perception?

2. When you hear the words "personal relationship with God," what is your reaction?

3. The author makes a distinction between religion—knowing *about* God—and spirituality or true faith—*knowing* God. What do you think of this distinction? Which describes your church's main concern?

4. Do you believe you can truly "know God"? Why or why not?

Action Step: Take a few minutes to record privately or share with someone where you are right now in your relationship to

God. What do you hope to get out of this book? How would you like to grow in God?

CHAPTER 1: CREATION: GOD REVEALS HIMSELF TO ALL

1. What has been your experience of God's revelation through nature? How important is nature to you in understanding what God is like?

2. What have you done in your life to bring yourself into contact with creation? What would you like to do more of?

3. What do you do for recreation? Does it truly renew as deeply as you'd like? Are there things you can do in nature that would satisfy you more?

4. What things can be learned about God's nature through creation? What things can't be known?

Action Step: In the coming week, do one thing to put yourself in direct contact with nature in some way. As you do so, pray that God would help you see more of him through the experience.

CHAPTER 2: THE WORD: GOD REVEALS HIMSELF TO THE MIND

1. The author states that idolatry—creating God in an image other than the way he's revealed himself—is deeply ingrained in human beings. Do you agree or disagree? What are some of the distorted images of God you have encountered, either personally or through what others have described?

2. What role does the Bible play in forming our concept of God? Why is this so important?

3. What difficulties have you encountered in understanding the Bible? How do you handle these difficulties?

4. What have been the most meaningful portions of Scripture to you? Which of the learning style(s) mentioned strike a chord in you? Do you see a correlation between the two?

Action Step: Incorporate the new approach to Bible study that attracts you most. Record or share any fresh insights.

CHAPTER 3: THE CHURCH: GOD REVEALS HIMSELF HUMANLY

1. How has God used other believers in a significant way in your life? Share specific incidents and how they affected you. Conversely, how has God used you in a tangible way to "bring God" to another person? What happened? How did what you did or said make God more real to you?

2. What are some of the ways you need other people? What tendencies from your own personality or background or current culture hinder you from allowing others to meet your needs?

3. What have you learned of God from other people's experiences of him? Is there anyone whose concept or experience of God bothers you? Why?

4. Which of the suggested ways of listening to God through others have been especially helpful to you? Which new ones would you like to try?

Action Step: Identify one of the people that God has used, or continues to use, regularly in your life. Write that person a note of gratitude for the input (if he or she is alive). Maintain an attitude of openness to that person in the coming days.

CHAPTER 4: GOD SPEAKS PERSONALLY

1. What are some of the various ways God revealed himself to individuals in the Bible? Do you believe he still uses a variety of means to reveal himself today? Why or why not?

2. The author points out several things God wants us to know about himself, about ourselves, about how God feels about us. What are some of the things you have learned in each of these areas?

3. Why is it so important to grasp the extent of God's love for us as individuals? How have you experienced that love so far?

4. Which of the various "love languages" mentioned are important to you in your human relationships? Do you also find God revealing himself to you in similar ways?

Action Step: Take a few minutes to reflect on how and when you feel most loved by God.

CHAPTER 5: TRACING YOUR SPIRITUAL AUTOBIOGRAPHY

1. Do you agree with the statement, "God is as creative in how he breaks into our lives as he is in the original creation"? Why or why not?

2. Why is it so important to remember specific times when God has been especially real to us?

3. The author suggests a process of tracing personal experiences of God's grace. Share one such instance with the group—perhaps your first impression of God—either verbally or by showing what you've done using one of the methods suggested. Describe the experience, the significance of that experience, your image of God from that experience, and your response.

4. After all who want to have shared their first impressions of God, spend some time praising God for the ways he has revealed himself in each other's lives.

Action Step: Begin your spiritual autobiography, as suggested in the chapter.

CHAPTER 6: FINDING GOD IN YOUR CIRCUMSTANCES

1. What are some of the ways God worked through the circumstances of human history as found in the Bible?

2. What are some of the ways God may use circumstances in our lives today? Which of these have you experienced?

3. Recall and share an instance in which you specifically sought God in a particular circumstance. Describe the circumstance and what you did. What did you learn about God through that situation?

4. When is it hardest to seek God—during difficult circumstances, times of spiritual dryness, times when things are going well, or times when life just drones along? Do you tend to actively seek God during such times?

Action Step: Most of us have experienced situations in which our sense of where God was at the time has never been resolved. Such experiences may block us from trusting God fully.

If this is true for you, begin to pray through the situation, seeking God until you sense some kind of resolution. This may come from a new perspective, from a new sense of assurance from Scripture, or some other revelation. The point is not to let anything from your past interfere with your current search for a deeper relationship with God.

CHAPTER 7: SEEKING GOD

1. The author opens this chapter with a story of how God used a particular everyday incident in her own life to teach her things about himself, herself, and her situation. If you can, share a similar experience from your own life—an everyday situation in which you sought God and sensed his working in some way.

2. Do you agree that we should seek God in everything we experience? Why or why not?

3. The author lists several things that can hinder us from hearing the voice of God. Are there any you disagree with? Would you add any? What hinders you most from tuning in to God's messages in your everyday life?

4. The author lists several attitudes that, when cultivated, enable us to hear God speaking in our personal lives. Which of these are easiest for you? Which are hardest?

Action Step: Choose the one thing that hinders you from hearing God and offer it to him to change. Tell someone how he is helping you in this area, or track it in a journal.

CHAPTER 8: HOW TO TUNE IN TO GOD

1. What interferes most with your taking time to tune in to God daily? What can you begin to do differently?

2. How have you experienced God communicating to you through your natural strengths and preferences? If you know or suspect your Myers-Briggs personality preferences, talk about how your preferences affect your spirituality.

3. The author mentions several other ways to look for and listen to God. Has God ever used any of these means to speak to you in the past?

4. Which of the areas discussed—key questions, key Scriptures, key images, opportunities for service, circumstances or relationships—seems most important at this time? How is God using this to show you more about himself?

Action Step: Choose one of the suggested methods for tuning in to God's voice as something you want to focus on now. In the coming days, record what happens.

CHAPTER 9: MAPPING YOUR SPIRITUAL DEVELOPMENT

1. The author states, "God often speaks to us through our strengths, [but] he *works in us* through our weaknesses." Do you agree with each part of this statement? Why or why not?

2. What are some of the ways God has come to you in your weakness?

3. What has kept you from facing your weaknesses in the past? How can you overcome that and bring even these areas to God?

4. How might strengths become liabilities? What can we do when we perceive this kind of weakness in our spiritual lives?

Action Step: Follow the suggestions under "Mapping Your Spiritual Development."

CHAPTER 10: LOVING GOD IN YOUR OWN LANGUAGE

1. What do the images "God is light" and "You are the light of the world" suggest to you?

2. Where do you find the most joy in your service to God? As you share your answer, other people from the group may want to confirm your gifts in that area.

3. Are there any areas of service in which you do not experience any joy? Solicit feedback from the group on whether your gifts are truly being used in that position. Is this a case of misplaced service, or are there other factors that are making the situation difficult?

4. Have you ever experienced a situation in which it has taken courage to respond to God in your own unique way? How has God supported you in that?

Action Step: If you are not sure of your particular means of loving God, go through the suggestions outlined in the chapter. If you do know, ask God to open one new door of opportunity to use your gift or express your love in your circumstances.

CHAPTER 11: OPEN TO GOD, OPEN TO OTHERS, OPEN TO GROWTH

1. The author suggests three images for our life with God: It is an adventure, requiring us to always be open to God's surprises and new directions. It is a journey, in which we're always on our way, never quite home in this world. And it is a dance. Which of these images speaks most to your experience, and why?

2. Share some of your personal experiences of how God has taken the initiative in your life.

3. The author talks about the place of death in the Christian life. What wrong images of God have you had to let die? How have you seen God transform some area of your life into something new?

4. What do the images of our becoming like little children, and our being the sheep of God's pasture, suggest to you?

Action Step: Ask God to reveal one new way he wants you to open yourself to him. Follow his lead.

NOTES

CHAPTER 1: CREATION: GOD REVEALS HIMSELF TO ALL

1. W. Phillip Keller, *Outdoor Moments with God* (Grand Rapids: Kregel Publications, 1994), 109–10.

2. Frank Laubach, *Letters by a Modern Mystic* (Westwood, N.J.: Fleming H. Revell Company, 1937, 1958), 28.

3. Quoted from "The Carrs' Courier," World Harvest Mission, April 1994.

4. Annie Dillard, *Pilgrim at Tinker Creek* (New York: Bantam, 1974), 6–8.

CHAPTER 2: THE WORD: GOD REVEALS HIMSELF TO THE MIND

1. For more about multiple intelligences theory, I recommend: *Frames of Mind* by Howard Gardner (New York: Basic Books, 1983); *Seven Kinds of Smart* (New York: Penguin, 1993) and *In Their Own Way* (New York: Putnam, 1987) by Thomas Armstrong.

2. I talk about energized abilities in my book, *A Life You Can Love* (Grand Rapids: Zondervan, 1995).

3. For those seeking guidance in the contemplative tradition, Richard Foster has some excellent suggestions for meditation and Bible study in *Celebration of Discipline* (San Francisco: Harper & Row, 1988). I also recommend Foster's *Prayer: Finding the Heart's True Home* (San Francisco: HarperSanFrancisco, 1992). Also very helpful: James Bryan Smith's *A Spiritual Formation Workbook* (San Francisco: HarperSanFrancisco, 1991) and *Spiritual Classics,* coedited with Richard Foster (New York: Harper Collins, 1990). *Journaling with Jeremiah* by Elizabeth Canham (New York: Paulist Press, 1992) also has some good suggestions for journaling through Scripture.

CHAPTER 3: THE CHURCH: GOD REVEALS HIMSELF HUMANLY

1. Rueben Welch, *We Really Do Need Each Other* (Nashville: Thomas Nelson, 1973), 34.

2. David Hazard, "Seeing More of God," *Discipleship Journal*, Jan./Feb. 1995, 46.

CHAPTER 4: GOD SPEAKS PERSONALLY

1. For further study on the names of God, I highly recommend Kay Arthur's book, *Lord, I Want to Know You* (Grand Rapids: Fleming H. Revell, 1984). Also, a great classic about the character of God is J. I. Packer's *Knowing God* (Downers Grove, Ill.: InterVarsity Press, 1973).

I have also found it very helpful to take some of the key images for God—Father, rock, fortress, shepherd—and trace them throughout the Bible, using a concordance. Another rich study would be to look at the New Testament for names and images for each member of the God-head: Father, Son of Man, Good Shepherd, Comforter, Advocate.

2. Judson J. Swihart, *How Do You Say, "I Love You"?* (Downers Grove, Ill.: InterVarsity Press, 1979), 15.

3. These are the "love languages" identified by Judson Swihart. Dr. Gary Chapman, in his book *The Five Love Languages* (Chicago: Moody Press, 1992), discusses touch, giving gifts, spending time with, words of affirmation, and acts of service.

CHAPTER 5: TRACING YOUR SPIRITUAL AUTOBIOGRAPHY

1. John Trent, *LifeMapping* (Colorado Springs: Focus on the Family, 1994). See especially chapter 4.

2. Ernest Boyer, Jr., *Finding God at Home* (San Francisco: Harper & Row, 1984), 41, 54.

CHAPTER 6: FINDING GOD IN YOUR CIRCUMSTANCES

1. Quoted from radio program Midday Connection, May 17, 1995.

2. Dr. Dan Allender and Tremper Longman III, *Cry of the Soul* (Colorado Springs: NavPress, 1994), 151–152.

CHAPTER 7: SEEKING GOD

1. Frank Laubach, *Learning the Vocabulary of God* (Nashville: The Upper Room, 1956), 9–10.

Chapter 8: How to Tune In to God

1. The information on type theory was drawn from the following books: *Gifts Differing,* by Isabel Briggs Myers (Palo Alto: Consulting Psychologists Press, 1980); *Please Understand Me,* by David Keirsey and Marilyn Bates (Del Mar, Calif.: Prometheus Nemesis, 1978); *Type Talk: The 16 Personality Types That Determine How We Live, Love and Work,* by Otto Kroeger and Janet M. Thuesen (New York: Delacorte Books, 1988); *Do What You Are,* by Paul D. Tieger and Barbara Barron-Tieger (Boston: Little, Brown and Company, 1992); *People Types and Tiger Stripes,* by Gordon Lawrence (Gainesville: Center for Applications of Psychological Type, 1982); *One of a Kind,* by LaVonne Neff (Gainesville: Center for Applications of Psychological Type, 1994); and *Mothers of Many Styles: A Personalized Profile of Your Mothering Style,* by Janet Penley and Diane Stephens (Wilmette, Ill.: Penley & Associates, Inc., 1995).

Chapter 9: Mapping Your Spiritual Development

1. Dallas Willard, *The Spirit of the Disciplines* (San Francisco: Harper & Row, 1988), 158.

Chapter 10: Loving God in Your Own Language

1. There are good lists in the current edition of *What Color Is Your Parachute?*, but even more detailed lists in *How to Create a Picture of Your Ideal Job or Next Career, Advanced Version* (revised) *of the Quick Job-Hunting (and Career-Changing) Map,* 1991, revised. Available from Ten Speed Press, Box 7123, Berkeley, CA 94707. Earlier editions of *Parachute* (early 1980s) include the aforementioned lists as well.

Some helpful resources, besides the Bolles book, are: Thomas Armstrong, *7 Kinds of Smart: Identifying and Developing Your Many Intelligences* (New York: Plume Books, 1993); Paul D. Tieger and Barbara Barron-Tieger, *Do What You Are* (Boston: Little, Brown, 1992), which is based on personality type; Ralph Mattson and Arthur Miller, *The Truth about You* (Berkeley, Calif.: Ten Speed Press, 1989); Lee Ellis and Larry Burkett, *Your Career in Changing Times* and *Finding the Career that Fits You* (Chicago: Moody Press, 1993). While all these focus on career skills, they are also skills that can be used in the context of serving God in other areas of life as well. My own book, *A Life You Can Love* (Grand Rapids: Zondervan, 1995), shows how to discover and integrate these kinds of skills into everyday life.

2. Ernest Boyer, Jr., *Finding God at Home* (San Francisco: Harper & Row, 1984), 49.

3. Sanna Anderson Baker, "Ordinary Loaves and Fishes," from *A Widening Light: Poems of the Incarnation*, Luci Shaw, editor (Wheaton, Ill.: Harold Shaw Publishers, 1984), 70–71. Used by permission of the author.

4. Boyer, 93, 108.

5. Henry T. Blackaby and Claude V. King, *Experiencing God* (Nashville: Broadman & Holman Publishers, 1994), 138.

CHAPTER 11: OPEN TO GOD, OPEN TO OTHERS, OPEN TO GROWTH

1. C. S. Lewis, *Prince Caspian* (New York: Macmillan, 1951), 150.

2. J. I. Packer, *Knowing God* (Downers Grove, Ill.: InterVarsity Press, 1973), 78–79.